Whillans
Tables

Seventy-second edition

Edited by
Gina Antczak FCA CTA
Kevin Walton BA (Hons)
Robert Wareham BSc (Econ) FCA

Members of the LexisNexis Group worldwide

United Kingdom	LexisNexis Butterworths, a Division of Reed Elsevier (UK) Ltd, Halsbury House, 35 Chancery Lane, LONDON, WC2A 1EL, and RSH, 1–3 Baxter's Place, Leith Walk EDINBURGH EH1 3AF
Argentina	LexisNexis Argentina, BUENOS AIRES
Australia	LexisNexis Butterworths, CHATSWOOD, New South Wales
Austria	LexisNexis Verlag ARD Orac GmbH & Co KG, VIENNA
Benelux	LexisNexis Benelux, AMSTERDAM
Canada	LexisNexis Canada, MARKHAM, Ontario
Chile	LexisNexis Chile Ltda, SANTIAGO
China	LexisNexis China, BEIJING and SHANGHAI
France	LexisNexis SA, PARIS
Germany	LexisNexis Deutschland GmbH, MUNSTER
Hong Kong	LexisNexis Hong Kong, HONG KONG
India	LexisNexis India, NEW DELHI
Italy	Giuffrè Editore, MILAN
Japan	LexisNexis Japan, TOKYO
Malaysia	Malayan Law Journal Sdn Bhd, KUALA LUMPUR
Mexico	LexisNexis Mexico, MEXICO
New Zealand	LexisNexis NZ Ltd, WELLINGTON
Poland	Wydawnictwo Prawnicze LexisNexis Sp, WARSAW
Singapore	LexisNexis Singapore, SINGAPORE
South Africa	LexisNexis Butterworths, DURBAN
USA	LexisNexis, DAYTON, Ohio

First published in 1948
© Reed Elsevier (UK) Ltd 2006
Published by LexisNexis Butterworths

All rights reserved. No part of this publication may be reproduced in any material form (including photocopying or storing it in any medium by electronic means and whether or not transiently or incidentally to some other use of this publication) without the written permission of the copyright owner except in accordance with the provisions of the Copyright, Designs and Patents Act 1988 or under the terms of a licence issued by the Copyright Licensing Agency Ltd, 90 Tottenham Court Road, London, England W1T 4LP. Applications for the copyright owner's written permission to reproduce any part of this publication should be addressed to the publisher.

Warning: The doing of an unauthorised act in relation to a copyright work may result in both a civil claim for damages and criminal prosecution.

Crown copyright material is reproduced with the permission of the Controller of HMSO and the Queen's Printer for Scotland. Parliamentary copyright material is reproduced with the permission of the Controller of Her Majesty's Stationery Office on behalf of Parliament. Any European material in this work which has been reproduced from EUR-lex, the official European Communities legislation website, is European Communities copyright.

A CIP Catalogue record for this book is available from the British Library.

ISBN for this volume
ISBN 10: 1 405 71115 9
ISBN 13: 9781405711159

Typeset by Phoenix Photosetting, Chatham, Kent
Printed and bound in Great Britain by CPI Bath Press, Bath
Visit LexisNexis Butterworths at www.lexisnexis.co.uk

Administration

Bank base rates

Period	Rate
From 3 August 2006	4.75%
4 August 2005–2 August 2006	4.5%
5 August 2004–3 August 2005	4.75%
10 June 2004–4 August 2004	4.5%
6 May 2004–9 June 2004	4.25%
5 February 2004–5 May 2004	4%
6 November 2003–4 February 2004	3.75%
10 July 2003–5 November 2003	3.5%
6 February 2003–9 July 2003	3.75%
8 November 2001–5 February 2003	4%
4 October 2001–7 November 2001	4.5%
18 September 2001–3 October 2001	4.75%
2 August 2001–17 September 2001	5%
10 May 2001–1 August 2001	5.25%
5 April 2001–9 May 2001	5.5%
8 February 2001–4 April 2001	5.75%
10 February 2000–7 February 2001	6%
13 January 2000–9 February 2000	5.75%
4 November 1999–12 January 2000	5.5%
8 September 1999–3 November 1999	5.25%
10 June 1999–7 September 1999	5%
8 April 1999–9 June 1999	5.25%
4 February 1999–7 April 1999	5.5%
7 January 1999–3 February 1999	6%
10 December 1998–6 January 1999	6.25%
5 November 1998–9 December 1998	6.75%
8 October 1998–4 November 1998	7.25%
4 June 1998–7 October 1998	7.5%
6 November 1997–3 June 1998	7.25%
7 August 1997–5 November 1997	7%
10 July 1997–6 August 1997	6.75%
6 June 1997–9 July 1997	6.5%
6 May 1997–5 June 1997	6.25%
30 October 1996–5 May 1997	6%
6 June 1996–29 October 1996	5.75%
8 March 1996–5 June 1996	6%
19 January 1996–7 March 1996	6.25%
13 December 1995–18 January 1996	6.5%
2 February 1995–12 December 1995	6.75%
7 December 1994–1 February 1995	6.25%
12 September 1994–6 December 1994	5.75%
8 February 1994–11 September 1994	5.25%
23 November 1993–7 February 1994	5.5%
26 January 1993–22 November 1993	6%
13 November 1992–25 January 1993	7%
16/19 October 1992–12 November 1992	8%
22 September 1992–15 October 1992	9%
17/18 September 1992–21 September 1992	10%
16 September 1992–16 September 1992	12%
5 May 1992–15 September 1992	10%

Due dates of tax

Capital gains tax
Normally 31 January following end of year of assessment. (TMA 1970 s 59B)
(See also *Extended due dates* under **Income tax**, below.)

Corporation tax
Generally
9 months and 1 day after end of accounting period. (FA 1998 Sch 19 para 29)

Instalments for larger companies (TMA 1970 s 59E, SI 1998/3175)
(A 'large company' is one whose taxable profits exceed £1.5m a year, divided by one plus the number of any active associated companies.)
    1st instalment: 6 months and 13 days from start of accounting period (or date of final instalment if earlier);
    (2nd instalment: 3 months after 1st instalment, if length of accounting period allows);
    (3rd instalment: 3 months after 2nd instalment, if length of accounting period allows);
    Final instalment: 3 months and 14 days from end of accounting period.

Transitional provisions percentage of total liability payable by instalments for accounting periods ending:
    after 30 June 1999 but before 1 July 2000: 60%
    after 30 June 2000 but before 1 July 2001: 72%
    after 30 June 2001 but before 1 July 2002: 88%
(balance due and payable in accordance with *Generally* above).

Close companies: tax on loans to participators
Loans etc made in accounting periods ending after 30 March 1996: 9 months and 1 day after the end of the accounting period. Previously 14 days after the end of the accounting period in which the loan was made. To be included in instalment payments for large companies (TMA 1970 s 59E(11), see above).

Income tax
Payments on account (TMA 1970 s 59A)
A payment on account is required where a taxpayer was assessed to income tax in the immediately preceding year to an amount exceeding the amount of tax deducted at source in respect of that year (subject to a de minimis limit, see below).
The payment on account is made in 2 equal instalments due on:
    (a)   31 January during the year of assessment, and
    (b)   31 July in the following year of assessment.
No payments on account are required where either:
    (a)   the aggregate of the liability (including Class 4 NIC) for the preceding year (net of tax deducted at source) is less than £500; or
    (b)   more than 80% of the taxpayer's income tax and Class 4 NIC liability for the preceding year was met by tax deducted at source (including PAYE).

Final payment (TMA 1970 s 59B, Sch 3ZA)
Balance of income tax due for a year of assessment (after deducting payments on account, tax deducted at source and credits in respect of dividends, etc) is due on:
    31 January following end of year of assessment (TMA 1970 s 59B(4)).

Extended due dates:
    (a)   If a taxpayer has given notice of liability within 6 months of the end of the year of assessment (under TMA 1970 s 7), but a notice to make a return is not given until after 31 October following the end of the year of assessment, the due date is 3 months after the notice is given (TMA 1970 s 59B(3)).
    (b)   If tax is payable as a result of a taxpayer's notice of amendment, an HMRC notice of correction or an HMRC notice of closure following enquiry, in each case given less than 30 days before the due date (or the extended due date at (a) above), the due date is on or before the day following the end of a 30-day period beginning on the day on which the notice is given (TMA 1970 s 59B(5), Sch 3ZA).
    (c)   If an assessment other than a self-assessment is made, tax payable under the assessment is due on the day following the end of a 30-day period beginning on the day on which notice of the assessment is given (TMA 1970 s 59B(6)).
The extensions under (b) and (c) do *not* alter the due date for *interest purposes* (see p 5).

Interest on overdue tax see p 5.   **Repayment supplement** see p 8.
Remission of tax see p 7.

Due dates of tax — continued

Inheritance tax

Chargeable transfers other than on death, made between:
6 April and 30 September — 30 April in next year.
1 October and 5 April — 6 months after end of month in which chargeable transfer is made.
Chargeable events following conditional exemption for heritage etc property and charge on disposal of trees or underwood before the second death
— 6 months after end of month in which chargeable event occurs.
Transfers on death
Earlier of (a) 6 months after end of month in which death occurs, and
(b) delivery of account by personal representatives.
Tax or extra tax becoming payable on death:
(1) chargeable transfers and potentially exempt transfers within 7 years of death, or
(2) gifts in excess of £100,000 made to political parties before 15 March 1988 and within 1 year of death: due 6 months after end of month in which death takes place.

PAYE and national insurance

Employer's tax and Class 1 national insurance payable under PAYE.	19 April following deduction year (extended to 22 April where payments after 5 April 2004 are made by electronic means).
Class 1A national insurance.	19 July following year in which contributions due.
PAYE settlement agreement and Class 1B national insurance.	19 October following year to which agreement relates.
Class 4 national insurance.	See under income tax on p 4.

Stamp duties see p 86.

Interest on overdue tax

Interest runs from the due date (see page 4) to the date of payment, on the amount outstanding. For tax resulting from amendments/corrections to returns and from discovery assessments (under TMA 1970 s 29), interest normally runs from the annual filing date for the relevant tax year.

Interest is payable gross and is not tax deductible.

Income tax, capital gains tax, NICs Class 1, 1A, 4 and (from 6.4.99) 1B, and (from 1.10.99) stamp duty, SDRT and (from 26.9.05) stamp duty land tax

Period	Rate
from 6 September 2005	6.5%
6 September 2004–5 September 2005	7.5%
6 December 2003–5 September 2004	6.5%
6 August 2003–5 December 2003	5.5%
6 November 2001–5 August 2003	6.5%
6 May 2001–5 November 2001	7.5%
6 February 2000–5 May 2001	8.5%
6 March 1999–5 February 2000	7.5%
6 January 1999–5 March 1999	8.5%
6 August 1997–5 January 1999	9.5%
31 January 1997–5 August 1997	8.5%
6 February 1996–30 January 1997	6.25%

Surcharge on unpaid income tax and capital gains tax (TMA 1970 s 59C)

Where income tax or capital gains tax becomes payable and all or part of it remains unpaid the day following 28 days after the due date, the taxpayer is liable to a surcharge of 5% of the unpaid tax. A further surcharge of 5% is levied on any of the tax remaining unpaid 6 months and 1 day from the due date. Interest is payable on surcharge from the expiry of 30 days beginning on the day on which the surcharge is imposed until the date of payment chargeable at the above rate.

Interest on overdue tax – continued

Corporation tax

Interest runs from the due date (see p 4) to the date of payment. For instalment payments by large companies for accounting periods ending after 30 June 1999, a special rate of interest runs from the due date to the earlier of the date of payment and nine months after the end of the accounting period (after which the normal rate applies).

Corporation tax self-assessment (accounting periods ending after 30 June 1999)

Period	Normal rate
from 6 September 2005	6.5%
6 September 2004–5 September 2005	7.5%
6 December 2003–5 September 2004	6.5%
6 August 2003–5 December 2003	5.5%
6 November 2001–5 August 2003	6.5%
6 May 2001–5 November 2001	7.5%
6 February 2000–5 May 2001	8.5%
6 March 1999–5 February 2000	7.5%

Period	Special rate for instalment payments (except where still unpaid nine months after end of accounting period)
from 14 August 2006	5.75%
15 August 2005–13 August 2006	5.5%
16 August 2004–14 August 2005	5.75%
21 June 2004–15 August 2004	5.5%
17 May 2004–20 June 2004	5.25%
16 February 2004–16 May 2004	5%
17 November 2003–15 February 2004	4.75%
21 July 2003–16 November 2003	4.5%
17 February 2003–20 July 2003	4.75%
19 November 2001–16 February 2003	5%
15 October 2001–18 November 2001	5.5%
1 October 2001–14 October 2001	5.75%
13 August 2001–30 September 2001	6%
21 May 2001–12 August 2001	6.25%
16 April 2001–20 May 2001	6.5%
19 February 2001–15 April 2001	6.75%
20 April 2000–18 February 2001	7%
21 February 2000–19 April 2000	8%
24 January 2000–20 February 2000	7.75%
15 November 1999–23 January 2000	7.5%

Corporation tax pay and file (accounting periods ending after 30 September 1993)

Period	Rate
from 6 September 2005	5.25%
6 September 2004–5 September 2005	6%
6 December 2003–5 September 2004	5.25%*
6 August 2003–5 December 2003	4.25%
6 November 2001–5 August 2003	5%
6 May 2001–5 November 2001	6%
6 February 2000–5 May 2001	6.75%
6 March 1999–5 February 2000	5.75%

* This rate was corrected by HMRC (see news release HMRC 27/05 of 6 September 2005) and is higher than that previously used (5%). No attempt will be made to recover any further interest which may be due unless, exceptionally, a liability is reviewed.

Income tax on company payments (due on or after 14 October 1999)

Period	Rate
from 6 September 2005	6.5%
6 September 2004–5 September 2005	7.5%
6 December 2003–5 September 2004	6.5%
6 August 2003–5 December 2003	5.5%
6 November 2001–5 August 2003	6.5%
6 May 2001–5 November 2001	7.5%
6 February 2000–5 May 2001	8.5%
14 October 1999–5 February 2000	7.5%

Inheritance tax

Interest runs from the due date (see page 5) to the date of payment.

Period	Rate
from 6 September 2005	3%
6 September 2004–5 September 2005	4%
6 December 2003–5 September 2004	3%
6 August 2003–5 December 2003	2%
6 November 2001–5 August 2003	3%
6 May 2001–5 November 2001	4%
6 February 2000–5 May 2001	5%
6 March 1999–5 February 2000	4%
6 October 1994–5 March 1999	5%
6 January 1994–5 October 1994	4%
6 December 1992–5 January 1994	5%
6 November 1992–5 December 1992	6%
6 July 1991–5 November 1992	8%
6 May 1991–5 July 1991	9%
6 March 1991–5 May 1991	10%

Remission of tax

By concession, arrears of tax may be waived if they result from HMRC's failure to make proper and timely use of information supplied by the taxpayer or, where it affects the taxpayer's coding, by his or her employer. The concession also applies to information supplied by the Department for Work and Pensions affecting the taxpayer's entitlement to a retirement or widow's pension (see Concession A19). The concession only applies where the taxpayer could reasonably have believed that his or her affairs were in order and (unless the circumstances are exceptional) where the taxpayer is notified of the arrears more than 12 months after the end of the tax year in which HMRC received the information indicating that more tax was due.

Interest on overpaid tax

Income tax, capital gains tax, Class 1, 1A, 4 and (from 6.4.99) 1B national insurance contributions and (from 1.10.99) stamp duty and stamp duty reserve tax and (from 26.9.05) stamp duty land tax

Calculated as simple interest on the amount of tax repaid. The supplement is tax free.
See pages 9 and 10 for rates applicable to corporation tax and page 86 with respect to stamp duties.

Period	Rate
from 6 September 2005	2.25%
6 September 2004–5 September 2005	3%*
6 December 2003–5 September 2004	2·25%*
6 August 2003–5 December 2003	1·5%*
6 November 2001–5 August 2003	2·25%*
6 May 2001–5 November 2001	3%*
6 February 2000–5 May 2001	4%
6 March 1999–5 February 2000	3%
6 January 1999–5 March 1999	4%
6 August 1997–5 January 1999	4·75%
6 February 1997–5 August 1997	4%
6 February 1996–5 February 1997	6·25%
6 March 1995–5 February 1996	7%
6 October 1994–5 March 1995	6·25%
6 January 1994–5 October 1994	5·5%
6 March 1993–5 January 1994	6·25%
6 December 1992–5 March 1993	7%
6 November 1992–5 December 1992	7·75%
6 October 1991–5 November 1992	9·25%
6 July 1991–5 October 1991	10%
6 May 1991–5 July 1991	10·75%
6 March 1991–5 May 1991	11·5%
6 November 1990–5 March 1991	12·25%

* These rates were corrected by HMRC (see news release HMRC 28/05 of 6 September 2005) and are higher than those previously used. No attempt will be made to recover amounts overpaid by HMRC unless, exceptionally, a repayment is reviewed.

Income tax
(TA 1988 s 824; FA 1997 s 92; ITTOIA 2005 s 749)
From 1996–97 (1997–98 for partnerships whose trade, profession or business commenced before 6 April 1994) repayment supplement applies to:
   (a) amounts paid on account of income tax
   (b) income tax paid by or on behalf of an individual
   (c) surcharges on late payments of tax
   (d) penalties incurred by an individual under any provision of TMA 1970
but excluding amounts paid in excess of the maximum the taxpayer is required to pay.
Except for tax deducted at source, the repayment supplement runs *from* the date on which the tax, penalty or surcharge was paid *to* the date on which the order for repayment is issued. For tax deducted at source, repayment supplement runs from 31 January after the end of the tax year for which the tax was deducted.

Capital gains tax
(TCGA 1992 s 283; FA 1997 s 92)
From 1996–97 repayment supplement runs *from* the date on which the tax was paid *to* the date on which the order for repayment is issued.

Inheritance tax
(IHTA 1984 s 235)
Repayments of inheritance tax or interest paid carries interest *from* the date of payment *to* the date on which the order for repayment is issued. The prescribed rates for unpaid tax apply equally to repayment supplements — see p 7.

Companies

Corporation tax self-assessment (accounting periods ending after 30 June 1999)

Normal rates
Rates on overpaid corporation tax in respect of periods after normal due date (SI 1989/1297 reg 3BB):

Period	Rate
from 6 September 2005	3%
6 September 2004–5 September 2005	4%
6 December 2003–5 September 2004	3%
6 August 2003–5 December 2003	2%
6 November 2001–5 August 2003	3%
6 May 2001–5 November 2001	4%
6 February 2000–5 May 2001	5%
6 March 1999–5 February 2000	4%

Special rates
For instalment payments by large companies and early payments by other companies, a special rate of interest runs from the date the excess arises (but not earlier than the due date of the first instalment) to the earlier of the date the repayment order is issued and 9 months after the end of the accounting period after which the normal rate of interest (as above) applies.

Rates on overpaid instalment payments and on corporation tax paid early (but not due by instalments):

Period	Rate
from 14 August 2006	4.5%
15 August 2005–13 August 2006	4.25%
16 August 2004–14 August 2005	4.5%
21 June 2004–15 August 2004	4.25%
17 May 2004–20 June 2004	4%
16 February 2004–16 May 2004	3.75%
17 November 2003–15 February 2004	3.5%
21 July 2003–16 November 2003	3.25%
17 February 2003–20 July 2003	3.5%
19 November 2001–16 February 2003	3.75%
15 October 2001–18 November 2001	4.25%
1 October 2001–14 October 2001	4.5%
13 August 2001–30 September 2001	4.75%
21 May 2001–12 August 2001	5%
16 April 2001–20 May 2001	5.25%
19 February 2001–15 April 2001	5.5%
21 February 2000–18 February 2001	5.75%
24 January 2000–20 February 2000	5.5%
15 November 1999–23 January 2000	5.25%
20 September 1999–14 November 1999	5%
21 June 1999–19 September 1999	4.75%
19 April 1999–20 June 1999	5%
15 February 1999–18 April 1999	5.25%
18 January 1999–14 February 1999	5.75%
7 January 1999–17 January 1999	6%

Interest on overpaid tax — continued

Corporation tax pay and file *(accounting periods ending before 1 July 1999)*
Repayments of corporation tax, repayments of income tax in respect of payments received, payments of tax credits in respect of franked investment income received, and (before its abolition from 6 April 1999) repayments of ACT in respect of foreign income dividends made after the material date. (FA 1998 ss 31, 32, SI 1999/358).

Calculated *from* the material date *to* the date the repayment order is issued.

For corporation tax, the material date is the later of
(a) the date on which the tax was paid and
(b) the date on which the tax became, or would have become, due and payable – generally, 9 months and 1 day after the end of the accounting period.

(For ACT, the material date was the date on which corporation tax for the accounting period in which the distribution was made became, or would have become, due and payable – generally, 9 months and 1 day after the end of the accounting period.)

For repayments of income tax in respect of payments received and payments of tax credits in respect of franked investment income received, the material date is the date on which corporation tax for the accounting period in which the payments or the franked investment income were received became, or would have become, due and payable. Again, this is generally 9 months and 1 day after the end of the accounting period.

Where there is in any accounting period ('the later period') a non-trading deficit on a company's loan relationships and a claim is made to carry this deficit back to an earlier accounting period ('the earlier period'), then interest on any repayment of corporation tax for the earlier period (or of income tax on a payment received in the earlier period) resulting from the claim begins to run only after the date on which the corporation tax for the *later* period (the period in which the non-trading deficit arose) became due and payable. (TA 1988 s 826(7C)).

A similar rule (s 826(7) repealed for accounting periods beginning on or after 6 April 1999) applied to the carry-back of surplus ACT as applies to the carry-back of a non-trading deficit.

Trading losses carried back for more than 12 months (s 826(7A), (7B))
Where a claim is made under TA 1988 s 393A(1) to set off a loss incurred in a later period against the profits of an earlier period not falling within the 12 months immediately preceding the later period, and
(a) a repayment of corporation tax in respect of that earlier period or a repayment of income tax in respect of a payment received in the earlier period; or
(b) following a claim under TA 1988 s 242 to include surplus franked investment income in profits available for set-off, a payment of the whole or part of the tax credit comprised in franked investment income of the earlier period,

is made, interest in respect of that part of the repayment due to the claim under TA 1988 s 393A(1) or TA 1988 s 242 (so far as it relates to the claim under s 393A(1)) begins to run only after the date on which the corporation tax in respect of the later period (the lossmaking period) became, or would have become, due and payable.

Period	Rate
from 6 September 2005	2%
6 September 2004–5 September 2005	2.75%
6 December 2003–5 September 2004	2%
6 August 2003–5 December 2003	1.25%
6 November 2001–5 August 2003	2%
6 May 2001–5 November 2001	2.75%
6 February 2000–5 May 2001	3.5%
6 March 1999–5 February 2000	2.75%
6 January 1999–5 March 1999	3.25%
6 August 1997–5 January 1999	4%
6 February 1996–5 August 1997	3.25%

Certificates of tax deposit

The Series 7 Prospectus came into operation on 1 October 1993.

Certificates are not available for purchase for use against corporation tax liabilities. Certificates are available to individuals, trustees, companies or other persons or bodies for the payment of any taxes or other liabilities listed in the schedule to the Prospectus. Minimum first deposit £2,000; subsequent deposits not less than £500. Interest is paid gross and is chargeable to tax. It will only be paid for the first 6 years of a deposit. A deposit bears interest for the first year at the rate in force at the time of the deposit and for each subsequent year at the rate in force on the anniversary of the deposit.

Date	Amount	Held for (mths in yr)	Pay't of tax %	Cashed %
6.4.01–10.5.01	Under £100,000	no limit	2	1
	£100,000 or over	under 1	2	1
		1–under 3	4.25	2.25
		3–under 6	4	2
		6–under 9	3.75	2
		9–12	3.5	1.75
11.5.01–2.8.01	Under £100,000	no limit	2	1
	£100,000 or over	under 1	2	1
		1–under 6	4	2
		6–12	3.75	2
3.8.01–18.9.01	Under £100,000	no limit	1.5	0.75
	£100,000 or over	under 1	1.5	0.75
		1–under 3	4	2
		3–12	3.75	1.875
19.9.01–4.10.01	Under £100,000	no limit	1.25	0.75
	£100,000 or over	under 1	1.25	0.75
		1–under 3	3.5	1.75
		3–under 9	3.25	1.75
		9–12	3	1.5
5.10.01–8.11.01	Under £100,000	no limit	1	0.5
	£100,000 or over	under 1	1	0.5
		1–under 3	3.25	1.75
		3–12	3	1.5
9.11.01–6.2.03	Under £100,000	no limit	0.5	0.25
	£100,000 or over	under 1	0.5	0.25
		1–under 3	2.75	1.5
		3–under 6	2.5	1.25
		6–12	2.25	1.25
7.2.03–10.7.03	Under £100,000	no limit	0.25	0
	£100,000 or over	under 1	0.25	0
		1–under 3	2.75	1.25
		3–under 9	2.25	1
		9–12	2	1
11.7.03–6.11.03	Under £100,000	no limit	0	0
	£100,000 or over	under 1	0	0
		1–under 3	2.50	1.25
		3–under 6	2.25	1
		6–12	2	1
7.11.03–5.2.04	Under £100,000	no limit	0.25	0
	£100,000 or over	under 1	0.25	0
		1–12	3	1.5
6.2.04–6.5.04	Under £100,000	no limit	0.5	0.25
	£100,000 or over	under 1	0.5	0.25
		1–12	3	1.5
7.5.04–10.6.04	Under £100,000	no limit	0.75	0.25
	£100,000 or over	under 1	0.75	0.25
		1–12	3.25	1.5
11.6.04–5.8.04	Under £100,000	no limit	1	0.5
	£100,000 or over	under 1	1	0.5
		1–under 3	3.75	1.75
		3–under 6	3.5	1.75
		6–12	3.75	1.75
6.8.04–4.8.05	Under £100,000	no limit	1.25	0.5
	£100,000 or over	under 1	1.25	0.5
		1–12	3.75	1.75
5.8.05–	Under £100,000	no limit	1	0.5
	£100,000 or over	under 1	1	0.5
		1–under 3	3.5	1.75
		3–under 6	3.25	1.5
		6–12	3	1.5

Penalties

Personal tax and corporation tax

Offence	Penalty
Failure to notify chargeability to income or capital gains tax within 6 months of tax year or to corporation tax within one year of accounting period (TMA 1970 s 7; FA 1998 Sch 18 para 2).	Up to tax liability still unpaid after 31 January following tax year (IT or CGT) or one year after end of accounting period (CT).
Failure to render return for income tax or capital gains tax (TMA 1970 ss 93, 93A).	(a) Initial penalty of £100 (or tax due if less); (b) upon direction by Commissioners, further penalty up to £60 for each day failure continues; (c) if failure continues after six months from filing date, and no penalty imposed under (b), a further penalty of £100 (or tax due if less); (d) if failure continues after one year from filing date, a further penalty up to amount of tax due.
Failure to render return for corporation tax (FA 1998 Sch 18 paras 17, 18).	(a) £100 if up to 3 months late (£500 if previous two returns also late); (b) £200 if over 3 months late (£1,000 if previous two returns also late); (c) if failure continues on final day for delivery of return or, if later, 18 months after return period, 10% of tax unpaid 18 months after return period (20% of tax unpaid at that date if return not made within two years of return period).
Failure to maintain records (TMA 1970 s 12B).	Up to £3,000.
Fraudulently or negligently making an incorrect statement in connection with a claim to reduce payments on account (TMA 1970 s 59A).	Up to the amount (or additional amount) payable on account if a correct statement had been made.
Fraudulently or negligently delivering incorrect return or accounts or making an incorrect claim for an allowance, deduction or relief (TMA 1970 ss 95, 95A; FA 1998 Sch 18 para 89).	Up to amount of tax underpaid by reason of incorrectness for (IT and CGT) the tax year (or following tax year and any preceding tax year) in which the return or claim is delivered, (CT) the accounting period(s) to which the return or claim relates.
Failure to remedy error discovered on an incorrect corporation tax return without unreasonable delay.	Up to amount of tax underpaid by reason of incorrectness for the accounting period to which the return or claim relates.
Failure to notify within charge to corporation tax within three months after the beginning of the first accounting period and any subsequent accounting period not following on immediately from the end of a previous accounting period. With effect for accounting periods beginning on or after 22 July 2004 (FA 2004 s 55).	(a) Initial penalty up to £300; and (b) a continuing penalty up to £60 for each day on which the failure continues.
Failure to register as self-employed (and liable to Class 2 NIC) within three months after the month in which self-employment begins (SI 2001/1004 reg 87).	Up to £100.

PAYE returns

Offence	Penalty
Failure to submit return P9D or P11D (benefits in kind) by due date (6 July following subsequent tax years) (TMA 1970 s 98(1)).	(a) Initial penalty up to £300; and (b) continuing penalty up to £60 for each day on which the failure continues.
Fraudulently or negligently submitting incorrect return P9D or P11D (TMA 1970 s 98(2)).	Penalty up to £3,000.
Failure to submit returns P14 (individual end of year summary), P35 (annual return), P38 or P38A (supplementary returns for employees not on P35) by due date (19 May following tax year) (TMA 1970 s 98A).	(a) First 12 months: penalty of £100 for each 50 employees (or part thereof) for each month the failure continues; (b) failures exceeding 12 months: penalty up to amount of PAYE or NIC due and unpaid after 19 April following tax year.
Fraudulently or negligently submitting incorrect forms P14, P35, P38 or P38A (TMA 1970 s 98A).	Penalty up to the amount of tax due.

PAYE returns — continued

Offence	Penalty
Failure to submit returns P11D(b) (Class 1A NIC returns) by due date (19 July following tax year, extended for 2000/01 only to 19 September 2001) (SI 2001/1004 reg 81).	(a) First 12 months: penalty of £100 for each 50 employees (or part thereof) for each month the failure continues (but total penalty not to exceed total Class 1A NIC due); (b) failures exceeding 12 months: a penalty not exceeding the amount of Class 1A NIC due and unpaid after 19 July following tax year.
Failure to submit information in connection with mandatory e-filing from 2004/05 onwards (SI 1993/744 as amended).	Penalty based on number of employees not exceeding £3,000 for 1,000 or more employees.

Inheritance tax returns and information

Offence	Penalty
Failure to deliver an account within 12 months of death (unless tax is less than £100 or there is a reasonable excuse) (IHTA 1984 s 245). [1] The fixed penalty in (a) and (c) relates to failures where the account is due by 22 January 2005 (FA 2004 s 295(5)). [2] Where the account is due on or before 22 July 2004, the penalty in (d) relates to failures continuing after 21 July 2005 (FA 2004 s 295(6)).	(a) Initial penalty of (up to)[1] £100 (or the amount of tax payable if less); (b) further penalty up to £60 (where penalty determined by court or Special Commissioners) for each day on which the failure continues; (c) if failure continues after six months after the date on which account is due, and proceedings not commenced, a further penalty of (up to)[1] £100 (or amount of tax payable if less); and (d) if failure continues one year after end of the period in which account is due (where the account is due after 22 July 2004)[2], and IHT is payable, a penalty not exceeding £3,000.
Failure to submit account or notify HMRC under IHTA 1984 s 218A if a disposition on a death is varied within 6 months of the variation and additional tax is payable (IHTA 1984 s 245A(1A)(1B)).	(a) Initial penalty up to £100; (b) further penalty up to £60 (if determined by court or Special Commissioners) for each day on which the failure continues; (c) up to £3,000 if failure continues after 12 months from date notification is due (where account due after 22 July 2004).
Failure to provide documents etc under IHTA 1984 s 219A(1) or (4) (IHTA 1984 s 245A(3)).	(a) Initial penalty up to £50; and (b) further penalty up to £30 (where penalty determined by court or Special Commissioners) for each day on which the failure continues.
Taxpayer fraudulently or negligently delivering, furnishing or producing incorrect accounts, information or documents (IHTA 1984 s 247; FA 2004 s 295(4)(9)).	(Accounts etc delivered after 22 July 2004) penalty up to the amount of tax payable. (Accounts etc delivered on or before 22 July 2004) (a) in the case of fraud, penalty up to aggregate of £3,000 and the amount payable; and (b) in the case of negligence, penalty up to the aggregate of £1,500 and the amount of tax payable.
Person other than the taxpayer fraudulently or negligently delivering, furnishing or producing incorrect accounts, information or documents (IHTA 1984 s 247(3); FA 2004 s 295(4)(9)).	(Accounts etc delivered after 22 July 2004) penalty up to £3,000. (Accounts etc delivered on or before 22 July 2004) (a) in the case of fraud, penalty up to £3,000; and (b) in the case of negligence, penalty up to £1,500.
Incorrect return etc: Assisting in or inducing the delivery, furnishing or production of any account, information or document knowing it to be incorrect (IHTA 1984 s 247(4).)	Up to £3,000.

Special returns of information

Offence	Penalty
Failure to comply with a notice to deliver a return or other document, furnish particulars or make anything available for inspection under any of the provisions listed in column 1 of the table in TMA 1970 s 98.	(a) Initial penalty up to £300 (£3,000 in relation to TA 1988 s 765A (movements of capital between residents of EU Member States); (b) further penalty up to £60 (£600) for each day on which the failure continues.
Failure to furnish information, give certificates or produce documents or records under any of the provisions listed in column 2 of the table in TMA 1970 s 98.	(a) Initial penalty up to £300; and (b) further penalty up to £60 for each day on which the failure continues.
Fraudulently or negligently delivering any incorrect document, information etc required under the above provisions.	Penalty up to £3,000.
Failure to deduct income tax at source from payments of interest or royalties under TA 1988 ss 349(1), 350(1) where the exemption does not apply and the company did not believe or could not reasonably have believed that it would apply (TMA 1970 s 98(4A)–(4D)).	(a) Initial penalty up to £3,000; and (b) further penalty up to £600 for each day on which the failure continues.
Advance pricing agreements: Fraudulently or negligently making a false or misleading statement in the preparation of, or application to enter into, any advance pricing agreement (FA 1999 s 86).	Penalty up to £10,000.

Other offences by taxpayers, agents etc

Offence	Penalty
Falsification of documents. Intentionally falsifying, concealing or destroying documents required under TMA 1970 ss 20, 20A or 20BA (TMA 1970 s 20BB).	On summary conviction, a fine up to the statutory maximum (£5,000); on conviction on indictment, imprisonment for a term not exceeding 2 years or a fine or both.
Failure to produce documents etc for the purposes of an enquiry under TMA 1970 s 19A or under FA 1998 Sch 18 para 27 (TMA 1970 s 97AA; FA 1998 Sch 18 para 29).	(a) Initial penalty of £50; and (b) further penalty up to £30 (if determined by HMRC) or £150 (if determined by Commissioners) for each day on which failure continues.
European Economic Interest Groupings— Offences in connection with the supply of information:	
(i) failure to supply information	Initial penalty up to £300 per member of the Grouping at the time of failure and after direction by the Commissioners: continuing penalty up to £60 per member of the Grouping at the end of the day for each day on which the failure continues.
(ii) fraudulent or negligent delivery of an incorrect return, accounts or statement (TMA 1970 s 98B).	Up to £3,000 for each member of the Grouping at the time of delivery.
Assisting in the delivery of incorrect returns, accounts or information (TMA 1970 s 99).	Penalty up to £3,000.
Certificates of non-liability to income tax: Fraudulently or negligently giving such a certificate for the purposes of receiving interest gross on a bank or building society account, or failing to comply with an undertaking given in such a certificate (TMA 1970 s 99A).	Penalty up to £3,000.
Refusal to allow a deduction of income tax at source (TMA 1970 s 106).	£50.

Other offences by taxpayers, agents etc — continued

Offence	Penalty
Obstruction of officer in inspection of property to ascertain its market value (TMA 1970 s 111).	Up to £50.
Construction Industry Scheme: Failure by contractor to check validity of registration card (TA 1988 s 566(2B)–(2E)).	Up to £3,000.
Fraudulent attempt by sub-contractor to obtain or misuse a sub-contractor's certificate (TA 1988 s 561(10)(11)).	Up to £3,000.
Witnesses before Commissioners: Neglect or refusal to appear before Commissioners or refusal to be sworn or answer questions (SI 1994/1812).	Up to £1,000.
Fraudulent evasion of income tax (FA 2000 s 144).	On summary conviction, imprisonment for up to 6 months or a fine up to the statutory maximum (£5,000); on conviction on indictment, imprisonment for up to 7 years or a fine or both.
Enterprise investment scheme relief: Issue by a company of a certificate of approval for such relief fraudulently or negligently or without the authority of HMRC (TA 1988 s 306(6)).	Not exceeding £3,000.
Treasury consent: Creation or transfer of shares or debentures in a non-resident subsidiary company without the consent of HM Treasury (TA 1988 s 766).	On conviction on indictment— (a) imprisonment for not more than 2 years or a fine, or both; or (b) in the case of a UK company, a fine not exceeding the greater of £10,000, or three times the tax payable by the company attributable to income and gains arising in the previous 36 months.
Deliberately or recklessly failing to pay corporation tax due in respect of total liability of company for accounting period, or fraudulently or negligently making claim for repayment (TMA 1970 s 59E(4); SI 1998/3175 reg 13).	Penalty not exceeding twice amount of interest charged under SI 1998/3175 reg 7.
Failure of a company to maintain records (other than those only required for claims, etc, or dividend vouchers and certificates of income tax deducted where other evidence is available) (FA 1998 Sch 18 para 23).	Penalty not exceeding £3,000.
Failure to notify notifiable proposals or notifiable arrangements, or failure to notify the client of the relevant scheme reference number under the provisions of FA 2004 ss 308(1)(3), 309(1), 310 or s 312(1).	(a) An initial penalty not exceeding £5,000; (b) a continuing penalty not exceeding £600 for each day on which the failure continues after imposition of initial penalty.

Failure to notify scheme reference number etc. under FA 2004 s 313(1);
    for second failure, occurring within three years from the date on which the first failure began;
 	
    for subsequent failures, occurring within three years from the date on which the previous failure began.
[TMA 1970 s 98C; FA 2004 s 315(1)].
	Penalty of £100 in respect of each scheme to which the failure relates;
	    penalty of £500 in respect of each scheme to which the failure relates;
	
	    penalty of £1,000 in respect of each scheme to which the failure relates.

Mitigation of penalties

HMRC have discretion to mitigate or entirely remit any penalty or to stay or compound any penalty proceedings (TMA 1970 s 102).

Interest on penalties

Penalties under TMA 1970 Parts II (ss 7–12B), IV (ss 28A–43B), VA (ss 59A–59D) and X (ss 93–107) carry interest at the prescribed rate (see p 14): TMA 1970 s 103A. Surcharges on unpaid income tax and capital gains tax carry interest under TMA 1970 s 59C.

Stamp duties see p 86.

VAT see p 93.

Time limits for claims and elections

Whenever possible, a claim or election must be made on the tax return or by an amendment to the return (TMA 1970 s 42 and FA 1998 Sch 18 paras 9, 10, 67 and 79). Exceptions to this general rule are dealt with in TMA 1970 Sch 1A. Except where another period is expressly prescribed, a claim for relief in respect of income tax and capital gains tax must be made within five years from the 31 January following the year of assessment to which it relates (TMA 1970 s 43(1) as amended). The time limit for claims by companies remains at six years from the end of the accounting period to which it relates (TMA 1970 s 43(1) (b) and, for accounting periods ending after 1 July 1999, FA 1998 Sch 18 para 55).

The tables below set out some of the main exceptions to the general limits.

Income tax

Claim	Time limit
Trading losses: Loss sustained in a trade, profession or vocation to be set against other income of the year or the last preceding year. Extended to certain pre-trading expenditure by TA 1988 s 401 and ITTOIA 2005 s 57 (TA 1988 s 380(1)).	1 year after 31 January next following tax year in which loss arose.
Unrelieved trading losses to be set against capital gains (FA 1991 s 72, TA 1988 s 380(1)).	1 year after 31 January next following tax year in which loss sustained.
Losses of new trade etc: Loss sustained in the first 4 years of a new trade, profession or vocation to be offset against other income arising in the 3 years immediately preceding the year of loss. Extended to certain pre-trading expenditure by TA 1988 s 401 and ITTOIA 2005 s 57 (TA 1988 s 381(1)).	1 year after 31 January next following tax year in which loss sustained.
Property business losses: Claim for relief against total income (TA 1988 s 379A(3)).	1 year after 31 January next following tax year.
Loss on disposal of unlisted shares: Loss on disposal of shares in a qualifying trading company to be offset against other income of the year of loss or the last preceding year (TA 1988 s 574(1)).	1 year after 31 January next following tax year in which loss incurred.
Gift aid: Election to treat donations to charity under gift aid made after 5 April 2003 as made in the previous tax year (ITTOIA 2005 s 818).	On or before date on which donor delivers tax return for the previous tax year and not later than 31 January after that year.

Capital gains

Claim	Time limit
Assets of negligible value: Loss to be allowed where the value of an asset has become negligible (TCGA 1992 s 24(2)).	2 years after end of chargeable period of deemed sale (and reacquisition).
Assets held on 31 March 1982: Events occurring prior to 31 March 1982 to be ignored in computing gains arising after 5 April 1988 (TCGA 1992 s 35 (5), (6) as amended).	1 year after 31 January next following tax year in which first relevant disposal made after 5.4.88 (capital gains tax); 2 years after end of accounting period in which first relevant disposal made after 31.3.88 (corporation tax).
Main residence: Determination of main residence for principal private residence exemption (TCGA 1992 s 222(5)(a)).	2 years after acquisition of second residence.
Relief for loans to traders: Losses on certain loans to traders to be allowed as capital losses (TCGA 1992 s 253(3)).	2 years.
Relief for loans to traders (payments by guarantor): Losses arising from payments by guarantor of certain irrecoverable loans to traders to be allowed as capital losses at time of claim or 'earlier time' (TCGA 1992 s 253(4), (4A); FA 1996 s 135(2)).	5 years after 31 January following tax year in which payment made (capital gains tax); 6 years after end of accounting period in which payment made (corporation tax).
Election for valuation at 6 April 1965: Gain on a disposal of an asset held at 6 April 1965 to be computed as if the asset had been acquired on that date. An election once made is irrevocable (TCGA 1992 Sch 2 para 17).	1 year after 31 January following tax year in which disposal made (capital gains tax); 2 years after end of accounting period in which disposal made (corporation tax); or such further time as HMRC may allow.

Corporation tax

Claim	Time limit
Trading losses: Loss sustained by a company in a trade in an accounting period to be offset against profits of that accounting period and profits of the preceding year. Extended to certain pre-trading expenditure by TA 1988 s 401 (TA 1988 s 393A(1) (2A)(10)).	2 years or such further period as HMRC may allow.
Group relief: Group relief to be given for accounting periods ending after 30 June 1999. The surrendering company must consent to the claim (FA 1998 Sch 18 paras 66 to 77).	The last of: (a) 1 year from the filing date of the claimant company's return for the accounting period for which the claim is made; (b) 30 days after the end of an enquiry into the return; (c) if HMRC amend the return after an enquiry, 30 days after issue of notice of amendment; (d) if an appeal is made against the amendment, 30 days after the determination of the appeal; (or such later time as HMRC may allow).
Non-trading deficit on loan relationship: Claim for non-trading deficits on loan relationships (including non-trading debits on derivative contracts) in an accounting period ending after 30 September 2002 to be: (a) offset against profits of the same period or carried back (FA 1996 s 83, Sch 8 paras 1, 3); (b) treated as non-trading deficit of subsequent accounting period to be carried forward to succeeding accounting periods (FA 1996 s 83, Sch 8).	2 years after the end of the accounting period in which deficit arose (or such later time as HMRC may allow). 2 years after the end of that subsequent accounting period.
Intangible assets: Election to replace accounts depreciation with fixed writing-down allowance of 4% (FA 2002 Sch 29 para 10).	2 years after the end of the accounting period in which the asset was created or acquired.
Research and development: Claim for tax relief to be made, amended or withdrawn in the company tax return (or amended return) (FA 1998 Sch 18 paras 83E, 83LE).	1 year from the filing date for the return or such later time as HMRC may allow.
UITF 40 spreading adjustment: Election to treat it as arising and charged in an accounting period rather than spreading it over three to six years (FA 2006, Sch 15 para 13).	1 year from the filing date for the return.

Capital allowances

Claim	Time limit
Corporation tax claims (accounting periods ending after 30 June 1999): Claims, amended claims and withdrawals of claims in respect of corporation tax capital allowances for accounting periods ending after 30 June 1999 (CAA 2001 s 3(2), (3)(*b*), FA 1998 Sch 18 para 82).	The last of: (a) 1 year after the filing date of the claimant company's return for the accounting period for which the claim is made; (b) 30 days after the end of an enquiry into the return; (c) if HMRC amend the return after an enquiry, 30 days after issue of notice of amendment; (d) if an appeal is made against the amendment, 30 days after the determination of the appeal; (or such later time as HMRC may allow).
Plant and machinery: Claim for writing-down allowance where first-year allowance not claimed (CAA 1990 s 25(3), (3A)).	1 year after 31 January after tax year in which chargeable period ends (IT); 2 years after end of chargeable period (CT).
Short life assets: Plant or machinery to be treated as a short life asset (CAA 2001 s 85(2)).	1 year after 31 January after tax year in which chargeable period ends (IT); 2 years after end of chargeable period (CT).
Connected persons: Succession to a trade between connected persons to be ignored in computing capital allowances (CAA 2001 s 266).	2 years after the date of the succession.
Sales between persons under common control treated as made at the lower of open market value and tax written down value (CAA 2001 s 570(5)).	2 years after the date of the disposal.

Exchanges

Recognised stock exchanges

The following is a list of countries with exchanges which have been designated as recognised stock exchanges under TA 1988 s 841. Unless otherwise specified, any stock exchange (or options exchange) in a country listed below is a recognised stock exchange for the purposes of TA 1988 s 841, provided it is recognised under the law of the country concerned relating to stock exchanges.

The Revenue's interpretation of the phrase 'listed on a recognised stock exchange' and similar phrases is set out in its policy statement published on 27 November 2002. See HMRC Tax Bulletin 76, April 2005.

Country	Date of recognition
Australian Stock Exchange and its stock exchange subsidiaries	22 September 1988
Austria[3]	22 October 1970
Belgium[3]	22 October 1970
Brazil	
Rio De Janeiro Stock Exchange	17 August 1995
São Paulo Stock Exchange	11 December 1995
Canada	
Any stock exchange prescribed for the purposes of the Canadian Income Tax Act	22 October 1970
Cayman Islands Stock Exchange	4 March 2004
China	
Hong Kong – Any stock exchange recognised under Section 2A(1) of the Hong Kong Companies Ordinance	26 February 1971
Denmark	
Copenhagen Stock Exchange	22 October 1970
Finland	
Helsinki Stock Exchange	22 October 1970
France[3]	22 October 1970
Germany[3]	5 August 1971
Greece	
Athens Stock Exchange	14 June 1993
Guernsey[3]	10 December 2002
Iceland	31 March 2006
Irish Republic[3]	22 October 1970
Italy[3]	3 May 1972
Japan[3]	22 October 1970
Korea	10 October 1994
Luxembourg[3]	21 February 1972
Malaysia	
Kuala Lumpur Stock Exchange	10 October 1994
Malta Stock Exchange	29 December 2005
Mexico	10 October 1994
Netherlands[3]	22 October 1970
New Zealand	22 September 1988
Norway[3]	22 October 1970
Portugal[3]	21 February 1972
Singapore	30 June 1977
South Africa	
Johannesburg Stock Exchange	22 October 1970
Spain[3]	5 August 1971
Sri Lanka	
Colombo Stock Exchange	21 February 1972
Sweden	
Stockholm Stock Exchange	16 July 1985
Swiss Stock Exchange	12 May 1997
Thailand	10 October 1994
United Kingdom	6 April 1965
United States	
Any stock exchange registered with the Securities and Exchange Commission as a national securities exchange[1]	22 October 1970
Nasdaq Stock Market[2]	10 March 1992

[1] The term 'national securities exchange' does not include any local exchanges registered with the Securities and Exchange Commission.
[2] As maintained through the facilities of the National Association of Securities Dealers Inc and its subsidiaries.
[3] Any stock exchange which is a stock exchange within the meaning of the law of the country concerned relating to stock exchanges.

Recognised futures exchanges

The following is a list of exchanges which have been designated as recognised futures exchanges under TCGA 1992 s 288(6). By concession, those exchanges were recognised futures exchanges for the tax year of recognition onwards.

Recognised futures exchanges	Date of recognition
International Petroleum Exchange of London	6.8.85
London Metal Exchange	6.8.85
London Gold Market	12.12.85
London Silver Market	12.12.85
Chicago Mercantile Exchange	19.12.86
New York Mercantile Exchange	19.12.86
Philadelphia Board of Trade	19.12.86
Chicago Board of Trade	24.4.87
Mid America Commodity Exchange	29.7.87
Montreal Exchange	29.7.87
Hong Kong Futures Exchange	15.12.87
Commodity Exchange (Comex)	25.8.88
Sydney Futures Exchange	13.10.88
Euronext (London International Financial Futures and Options Exchange)	01.02
OM Stockholm	18.3.92
OM London	18.3.92
New York Board of Trade	10.6.04

Recognised investment exchanges and clearing houses

The following is a list of investment exchanges and clearing houses recognised as investment exchanges under the Financial Services and Markets Act 2000 and able to carry out investment business in the UK.

Recognised investment exchanges	Date of recognition
London Stock Exchange	22 November 2001
International Petroleum Exchange of London	5 April 1988
LIFFE Administration and Management	22 November 2001
London Metal Exchange	22 November 2001
Virt-x Exchange Ltd	23 November 2001
ICE Futures	22 November 2001
EDX London Ltd	1 July 2003
NYMEX Europe	7 September 2005
Recognised clearing houses	Date of recognition
CH Clearnet	23 November 2001
CRESTCo	23 November 2001

Recognised overseas investment exchanges and clearing houses

The following is a list of overseas investment exchanges and clearing houses recognised under the Financial Services and Markets Act 2000 and able to conduct investment business in the UK.

Recognised overseas investment exchange	Date of recognition
National Association of Securities Dealers Automated Quotations (NASDAQ)	23 November 2001
Sydney Futures Exchange	30 January 2002
Chicago Mercantile Exchange (CME)	23 November 2001
Chicago Board of Trade (CBOT)	23 November 2001
New York Mercantile Exchange (NYMEX)	23 November 2001
NQLX LLC	23 November 2001
Swiss Stock Exchange (SWX)	23 November 2001
Cantor Financial Futures Exchange (CFEE)	23 November 2001
EUREX Zurich	23 November 2001
Warenterminborse Hannover	23 November 2001
US Futures Exchange	21 May 2004
Recognised clearing house	Date of recognition
SIS x-clear AG	19 August 2004

Applications for clearances and approvals

Clearance application	Address
Transfer of long term insurance business (TCGA 1992 s 211, TA 1988 s 444A)	Both parties UK-resident: Robert Peel, Revenue Policy, Business Tax, 3rd Floor (3C/10), 100 Parliament Street, London SW1A 2BQ
	At least one party not UK-resident: Richard Thomas, Revenue Policy, Business Tax, 3rd Floor (3c/10), 100 Parliament Street, London SW1A 2BQ
Demergers (TA 1988 s 215); Company purchase of own shares (TA 1988 s 225); Transactions in securities (TA 1988 s 707); Enterprise Investment Scheme – acquisition of shares by new company (TA 1988 s 304A(1)(f)); Share exchanges (TCGA 1992 ss 138, 139, 140B, 140D); and Intangible fixed assets (FA 2002 Sch 29 para 88)	Clearance and Counteraction Team, Anti-Avoidance Group Intelligence, First Floor, 22 Kingsway, London WC2B 6NR (Market sensitive applications to Eric Gardner; non-market sensitive applications to Mohini Sawhney — see note below)[1]
Company migration (FA 1988 s 130)	Mike Bowen, Revenue Policy International, 100 Parliament Street, London SW1A 2BQ
Advance pricing agreements (FA 1999 ss 85–87)	Ian Wood, Revenue Policy International, 100 Parliament Street, London SW1A 2BQ
	For APAs involving oil taxation: Nic Perks or Malcolm Phelps, Revenue Policy, International, Oil Taxation Office (APAs), Melbourne House, Aldwych, London WC2B 4LL
Controlled foreign companies (TA 1988 ss 747–756, Schs 24–26)	Stephen Hewitt or Mary Sharp, Revenue Policy International, 100 Parliament Street, London SW1A 2BQ
Corporate Venturing Schemes (FA 2000 Sch 15)	Small Company Enterprise Centre, Centre for Revenue Intelligence (CRI), Ty Glas, Llanishen, Cardiff CF14 5ZG

Approval application	Address
Pensions (TA 1988 ss 590, 591)	HMRC, Pension Schemes Office, Yorke House, PO Box 62, Castle Meadow Road, Nottingham NG2 1BG
Employee share schemes (TA 1988 Sch 9)	Kevin Meehan, Revenue Policy, Capital and Savings, Employee Share Schemes, Second Floor, New Wing, Somerset House, London WC2R 1LB
Qualifying life assurance policies (TA 1988 Sch 15)	Claire Ritchie, Revenue Policy, Business Tax (Insurance), 3rd Floor (3C/09), 100 Parliament Street, London SW1A 2BQ
Professional bodies (relief for subscriptions) (TA 1988 s 201)	A list of approved professional bodies and learned societies is available on the HMRC website (at www.hmrc.gov.uk/list3/index.htm)

Application for treasury consent	Address
Transactions in shares or debentures (TA 1988 ss 765, 765A)	Andy Beazley, Doug Jones or Mary Sharp, Revenue Policy International, 100 Parliament Street, London SW1A 2BQ

Confirmation or pre-transaction advice	Address
Funding issues (TA 1988 ss 209, 703)	Andy Beazley, Revenue Policy International, 100 Parliament Street, London SW1A 2BQ
Transactions in land (TA 1988 ss 35, 776)	Applications for clearance should be sent to the Inspector of Taxes who deals with the returns

[1] Where clearance is sought under any one or more of TA 1988 ss 215, 225, 304A, 707; TCGA 1992 ss 138, 139, 140B, 140D; or FA 2002 Sch 29 para 88, clearance applications may be sent in a single letter to the above London address for clearances under those sections. The letter should make clear what clearance is required. E-mail applications can be sent to reconstructions@gtnet.gov.uk and fax applications to 020 7438 4409. For market sensitive information, call Eric Gardner on 020 7438 6585 before sending an e-mail or fax. A reply by e-mail should be requested if required. General enquiries can be made to Mohini Sawhney on 020 7438 8355.

Capital allowances

Rates

Agricultural and forestry land

	Expenditure incurred after	% Rate
Initial allowance	31 March 1986	Nil
	31 October 1992[1]	20
	31 October 1993	Nil
Writing-down allowance	31 March 1986	4

[1] Initial allowances were temporarily reintroduced for 1 year in respect of capital expenditure on agricultural buildings or works. The allowances applied to buildings or works constructed under a contract entered into between 1 November 1992 and 31 October 1993, and brought into use for the purposes of the farming trade by 31 December 1994. See CAA 1990 s 124A.

Dredging

	Expenditure incurred after	% Rate
Initial allowance	31 March 1986	Nil
Writing-down allowance	5 November 1962	4

Industrial buildings and structures

	Expenditure[1] incurred after	% Rate
Initial allowance		
Generally:	31 March 1986	Nil
	31 October 1992[2]	20
	31 October 1993	Nil
Exceptions:		
Enterprise zones	within 10 years of site being included in zone[3]	100
Writing-down allowance		
Generally:	5 April 1946	2
	5 November 1962[4]	4
Exception:		
Enterprise zones	within 10 years of site being included in zone[5]	25

[1] The amount qualifying for allowance is the price paid for the relevant interest *minus* (i) the value of the land element and (ii) any value attributable to elements over and above those which would feature in a normal commercial lease negotiated in the open market: FA 1995 s 100 confirming previous practice.
[2] Initial allowances were temporarily reintroduced for 1 year in respect of capital expenditure on industrial buildings and qualifying hotels. The allowances applied to buildings constructed under, or bought unused under, a contract entered into after 31 October 1992 and before 1 November 1993, and brought into use in qualifying trade by 31 December 1994. Balance of relief by 4% pa writing-down allowance. All or part of the initial allowance could be disclaimed. See CAA 1990 ss 2A, 10C.
[3] CAA 2001 s 306. Includes expenditure on qualifying hotels. See p 23 for enterprise zones.
[4] Includes expenditure on qualifying hotels (other than in an enterprise zone).
Also includes expenditure on the construction of toll roads incurred for accounting periods or basis periods ending after 5 April 1991.
[5] CAA 2001 s 310. Includes expenditure on qualifying hotels. See p 23 for enterprise zones.

Flat conversions

	Expenditure incurred after	% Rate
Initial allowance	10 May 2001	100

Applies to expenditure incurred on renovating or converting vacant or storage space above commercial properties to provide low value flats for rent. A writing-down allowance is given at 25% (on a straight-line basis) on unrelieved expenditure. (CAA 2001 ss 393A–393W; FA 2001 s 67, Sch 19).

Know-how

Expenditure incurred after 31 March 1986: annual 25% writing-down allowance (reducing balance basis).

Capital allowances: rates — continued

Plant and machinery

Expenditure incurred	after	before	% Rate
First-year allowance (FYA)[1]			
Small and medium-sized businesses[2]	1 July 1998		40
	1 July 1997	2 July 1998	50/12
in Northern Ireland *only*[3]	11 May 1998	12 May 2002	100
Small businesses[4]			
for income tax purposes	5 April 2006	6 April 2007	50
	5 April 2004	6 April 2005	50
for corporation tax purposes	31 March 2006	1 April 2007	50
	31 March 2004	1 April 2005	50
ICT[5]	31 March 2000	1 April 2004	100
Energy-saving plant or machinery[6]	31 March 2001		100
New low-emission cars and refuelling equipment[7]	16 April 2002	1 April 2008	100
Environmentally beneficial plant or machinery[8]	31 March 2003		100
Writing-down allowance (WDA)[9]			
Generally	26 October 1970		25
Leasing to non-residents[10]	9 March 1982	1 April 2006	10
Long-life assets[11]	25 November 1996		6

[1] **FYAs** available universally were abolished for expenditure after 31.3.86 but were reintroduced temporarily at the rate of 40% for expenditure in the year to 31.10.93. Thereafter, FYAs have been specifically targeted as below. Where given, they replace the WDA in the year of acquisition.

[2] **Small and medium-sized businesses:** The allowance does not apply to certain expenditure including that on plant and machinery for leasing, motor cars, ships, railway assets or long-life assets. After the first year, allowances revert to the normal WDA. The rate of 50% applied only for expenditure incurred during the year ended 1 July 1998 when a 12% FYA applied to long-life assets. (See notes 4 and 11 below.) Small and medium-sized businesses are, broadly, those satisfying any two of the following conditions: (*a*) turnover £22,800,000 or less (*b*) assets £11,400,000 or less (*c*) not more than 250 employees (CAA 1990 ss 22(3C)(6B), 22A, 44, 46–49). For accounting periods ending before 30.01.04, the thresholds were: (*a*) turnover £11,200,000 or less (*b*) assets £5,600,000 or less.

[3] The conditions for relief were similar to those outlined in note 2 above, but goods vehicles used in freight haulage businesses did not qualify (CAA 2001 ss 40–43, 46).

[4] **Small businesses:** See note 2 above for conditions for relief. Small businesses are, broadly, those satisfying any two of the following conditions: (*a*) turnover £5,600,000 or less (*b*) assets £2,800,000 or less (*c*) not more than 50 employees. For accounting periods ending before 30.01.04, the thresholds were: (*a*) turnover £2,800,000 or less (*b*) assets £1,400,000 or less. (FA 2004 s 142).

[5] *ICT (information and communications technology):* The allowances were available on buying computers or investing in e-commerce and new information technology. (CAA 2001 ss 45, 46).

[6] **Energy-saving plant or machinery:** The allowances are available for investment by *any* business in designated energy-saving plant and machinery in accordance with the Government's Energy Technology Product List (CAA 2001 ss 45A–45C, 46; FA 2001 s 65, Sch 17; SI 2001/2541; SI 2005/1114). The product lists are available at www.eca.gov.uk.

[7] **Low-emission cars:** The allowance is given on (*a*) new cars which are either electrically propelled or emit not more than 120g/km of carbon dioxide, registered after 16 April 2002 and (*b*) new plant and machinery to refuel vehicles with natural gas or hydrogen fuels (CAA 2001 ss 45D, 45E, 46).

[8] **Environmentally beneficial plant or machinery:** Allowances are available for expenditure by *any* business on new and unused designated technologies and products which satisfy the relevant environmental criteria in accordance with the Government's technologies or products lists (FA 2003 s 167, Sch 30). The product lists are available at www.eca.gov.uk.

[9] **WDAs** are calculated on a reducing balance basis. Generally, CAA 2001 s 56; leasing to non-residents, CAA 2001 s 109.

[10] The relief applies only to leases finalised before 1.4.06 (CAA 2001 s 109; FA 2006 Sch 9 para 13).

[11] **Long-life assets:** Applies to plant or machinery with an expected working life, when new, of 25 years or more. Applies where expenditure on long-life assets in a year is £100,000 or more (in the case of companies the de minimis limit is £100,000 divided by one plus the number of associated companies). Transitional provisions apply to maintain a 25% allowance for expenditure incurred before 1 January 2001 under a contract entered into before 26 November 1996 and to expenditure on second-hand plant or machinery if old rules applied to vendor. It does not apply to plant or machinery in a building used wholly or mainly as, or for purposes ancillary to, a dwelling-house, retail shop, showroom, hotel or office, cars, or sea-going ships and railway assets acquired before 1 January 2011 (CAA 2001 ss 90–104, Sch 3 para 20).

Cars: See p 23 and Car and motorcycle hire p 49.

Mineral extraction

First-year allowance: 100% FYA is available for certain expenditure incurred after 16 April 2002 wholly for the purposes of a North Sea Oil ring-fence trade or on plant and machinery used in such a trade.

Writing-down allowance: for expenditure incurred after 31 March 1986, 10% for expenditure on the acquisition of a mineral asset and certain pre-trading expenditure, otherwise 25% (on reducing balance basis).

(CA 2001 s 418)

Motor cars
available for private use

Writing-down allowance (WDA)	Expenditure incurred after 11 March 1992	% Rate 25%[1]

[1] Restricted to £3,000 for cars costing more than £12,000 and bought outright, on hire purchase or by way of a lease with an option to purchase (CAA 2001 ss 74, 75).
[2] The requirement that expenditure on cars costing £12,000 or less goes into a separate pool was removed from the start of the chargeable period which includes 1 April 2000 (corporation tax) or 6 April 2000 (income tax) or the start of the chargeable period which includes 1 (or 6) April 2001 at the option of the taxpayer (CAA 1990 s 41; FA 2000 s 74).
[1] See also note 7, p 22 and Car hire, p 49.

Patent rights
Writing-down allowance

Expenditure incurred after 31 March 1986: annual 25% writing-down allowance (reducing balance basis).
(CA 2001 s 472)

Research and development

(formerly scientific research)	Expenditure incurred after	% Rate
Allowance in year 1	5 November 1962	100

Note: Land and houses are excluded from 1 April 1985.
See also corporation tax relief, p 43.

Disadvantaged areas

Renovation of business premises

	Expenditure incurred after	% Rate
First-year allowance	Approval of state aid	100

The expenditure must be incurred on renovating or converting vacant business properties in the designated disadvantaged areas in the UK that have been vacant for at least a year to bring the property back into business use. The enhanced rate will apply to any expenditure currently qualifying for plant and machinery, industrial buildings or agricultural buildings allowances and also to expenditure on commercial buildings (such as shops and offices). A writing-down allowance is given at 25% (on a straight-line basis) on unrelieved expenditure. (FA 2005 s 92, Sch 6).

Enterprise zones

An initial allowance of 100% is available for expenditure on industrial or commercial building by businesses within enterprise zones. Where the initial allowance is not or is only partially claimed a 25% writing-down allowance on cost, on a straight-line basis, applies to the unclaimed balance.

The following areas have been designated as enterprise zones. The designation applies for 10 years from the commencement date. Previous enterprise zones, the designation of which has lapsed, are not shown.

Area	*Commencement date*
Tyne Riverside (North Tyneside) (No 2) (SI 1996/1981)	26 August 1996
Tyne Riverside (North Tyneside and South Tyneside) (SI 1996/2435)	21 October 1996

Capital gains

Annual exemption

Individuals, personal representatives[1] and certain trusts[2]

Exempt amount of net gains	2001–02	2002–03	2003–04	2004–05	2005–06	2006–07
	£7,500	£7,700	£7,900	£8,200	£8,500	£8,800

[1] Year of death and following 2 years (maximum).
[2] Trusts for mentally disabled persons and those in receipt of attendance allowance or disability living allowance. Exemption divided by number of qualifying settlements created (after 9 March 1981) by one settlor, subject to a minimum of one-tenth.

Trusts[1] generally

Exempt amount of net gains	2001–02	2002–03	2003–04	2004–05	2005–06	2006–07
	£3,750	£3,850	£3,950	£4,100	£4,250	£4,400

[1] Exemption divided by number of qualifying settlements created (after 6 June 1978) by one settlor, subject to a minimum of one-fifth.

Chattel exemption

	Disposals exemption	Marginal relief: Maximum chargeable gain
From 1989–90 onwards	£6,000	$\frac{5}{3}$ excess over £6,000

Rates of tax

2006–07	*Individuals*	
	• to income tax starting rate limit £2,150	10%
	• from £2,151 to income tax basic rate limit £33,300	20%
	• above income tax basic rate limit £33,300	40%
	Trusts and personal representatives	40%
2005–06	*Individuals*	
	• to income tax starting rate limit £2,090	10%
	• from £2,091 to income tax basic rate limit £32,400	20%
	• above income tax basic rate limit £32,400	40%
	Trusts and personal representatives	40%
2004–05	*Individuals*	
	• to income tax starting rate limit £2,020	10%
	• from £2,021 to income tax basic rate limit £31,400	20%
	• above income tax basic rate limit £31,400	40%
	Trusts and personal representatives	40%
2000–01 to 2003–04	*Individuals*	
	• to income tax starting rate limit	10%
	• above starting rate limit to income tax basic rate limit	20%
	• above income tax basic rate limit	40%
	Trusts and personal representatives	34%

Gains are taxed on individuals as the top slice of income. The above rates are subject to taper relief in certain cases. See page 26.

Trusts for vulnerable persons: From 2004–05 onwards, gains taxed at beneficiary's rates (on beneficiary if UK resident or on trustees if beneficiary not UK-resident).

Settlements where settlor retains an interest: chargeable on settlor at own rates.
Adjustment is necessary for savings income (including interest from banks and building societies, interest distributions from authorised unit trusts, interest from gilts and other securities including corporate bonds, purchased life annuities, and discounts). Adjustment is also necessary for dividends or other qualifying distributions from a UK-resident company.

Indexation allowance – individuals
(TCGA 1992 ss 53–57, 109)

For gains on disposals by individuals, trustees and personal representatives, an indexation allowance is given up to April 1998 and taper relief applies thereafter on disposals made after 5 April 1998 (see below). Indexation allowance is deducted before applying taper relief. The indexation allowance is calculated by multiplying each item of allowable expenditure by:

$$\frac{RD - RI}{RI}$$

where RD = Retail prices index figure for month of disposal
RI = Retail prices index for month of expenditure (or March 1982 if later)

See pages 30–41 for indexation allowances applicable for corporation tax and page 42 for RPI values.

For disposals after 31 March 1998 of assets acquired on or before that date the factors below can be used to calculate the indexation allowance available to April 1998 for acquisitions in the month shown.

	Jan	Feb	Mar	Apr	May	Jun	Jul	Aug	Sep	Oct	Nov	Dec
1982	–	–	1·047	1·006	0·992	0·987	0·986	0·985	0·987	0·977	0·967	0·971
1983	0·968	0·960	0·956	0·929	0·921	0·917	0·906	0·898	0·889	0·883	0·876	0·871
1984	0·872	0·865	0·859	0·834	0·828	0·823	0·825	0·808	0·804	0·793	0·788	0·789
1985	0·783	0·769	0·752	0·716	0·708	0·704	0·707	0·703	0·704	0·701	0·695	0·693
1986	0·689	0·683	0·681	0·665	0·662	0·663	0·667	0·662	0·654	0·652	0·638	0·632
1987	0·626	0·620	0·616	0·597	0·596	0·596	0·597	0·593	0·588	0·580	0·573	0·574
1988	0·574	0·568	0·562	0·537	0·531	0·525	0·524	0·507	0·500	0·485	0·478	0·474
1989	0·465	0·454	0·448	0·423	0·414	0·409	0·408	0·404	0·395	0·384	0·372	0·369
1990	0·361	0·353	0·339	0·300	0·288	0·283	0·282	0·269	0·258	0·248	0·251	0·252
1991	0·249	0·242	0·237	0·222	0·218	0·213	0·215	0·213	0·208	0·204	0·199	0·198
1992	0·199	0·193	0·189	0·171	0·167	0·167	0·171	0·171	0·166	0·162	0·164	0·168
1993	0·179	0·171	0·167	0·156	0·152	0·153	0·156	0·151	0·146	0·147	0·148	0·146
1994	0·151	0·144	0·141	0·128	0·124	0·124	0·129	0·124	0·121	0·120	0·119	0·114
1995	0·114	0·107	0·102	0·091	0·087	0·085	0·091	0·085	0·080	0·085	0·085	0·079
1996	0·083	0·078	0·073	0·066	0·063	0·063	0·067	0·062	0·057	0·057	0·057	0·053
1997	0·053	0·049	0·046	0·040	0·036	0·032	0·032	0·026	0·021	0·019	0·019	0·016
1998	0·019	0·014	0·011	–	–	–	–	–	–	–	–	–

Losses. For disposals after 30 November 1993, indexation allowance can only be used to reduce or extinguish a gain. It cannot be used to create or increase a capital loss.

Share identification rules
(TCGA 1992 ss 104–106A; FA 2006 s 74)

For acquisitions before 6 April 1998 and for acquisitions on or after that date, for corporation tax on capital gains purposes, shares and securities of the same class in the same company are pooled and treated as a single asset.

For acquisitions after 5 April 1998 for individuals, trustees and personal representatives, disposals are identified with acquisitions in the following order:
- same day acquisitions (subject to special rules distinguishing shares acquired after 5 April 2002 from approved employee share option schemes from other shares acquired on the same day);
- acquisitions within the following 30 days[1] (thus countering 'bed and breakfasting');
- previous acquisitions after 5 April 1998 on a last in/first out basis;
- shares acquired after 5 April 1982 in the pool at 5 April 1998 (the 'section 104 holding');
- shares acquired before 6 April 1982 (the '1982 holding');
- any shares acquired on or before 6 April 1965 on a last in/first out basis;
- if any shares disposed of are still not fully matched, shares acquired subsequent to the disposal (beyond the above mentioned 30-day period).

[1] The 30-day matching rule does not apply in relation to acquisitions after 21 March 2006 where the individual making the disposal is not (or is not treated as) resident or ordinarily resident in the UK at the time of the acquisition.

Taper relief

(TCGA 1992 s 2A, Sch A1; FA 2000 ss 66, 67; FA 2002 ss 46, 47, Sch 10; FA 2003 s 160)

Taper relief is available for disposals made after 5 April 1998 by individuals, trustees and personal representatives. The chargeable gain is reduced according to the number of complete years for which the asset has been held (counting from 6 April 1998). Non-business assets acquired before 17 March 1998 qualify for an addition of one year to the period for which they are held after 5 April 1998. Business assets acquired before 17 March 1998 also qualify for the one-year addition but only if disposed of before 6 April 2000.

Taper relief applies to gains after all deductions and before the annual exemption. Losses are set against pre-tapered gains in the most beneficial way possible. Where applicable, the combined period of holding by spouses is taken into account.

Business assets			
Disposals from 6 April 2002		Disposals from 6 April 2000 to 5 April 2002	
No of complete yrs from 6.4.98 for which asset held	% of gain chargeable	No of complete yrs from 6.4.98 for which asset held	% of gain chargeable
0	100	0	100
1	50	1	87.5
2 or more	25	2	75
		3	50
		4 or more	25

Non-business assets			
No of complete yrs from 6.4.98 for which asset held	% of gain chargeable	No of complete yrs from 6.4.98 for which asset held	% of gain chargeable
0	100	6	80
1	100	7	75
2	100	8	70
3	95	9	65
4	90	10 or more	60
5	85		

Business assets. A 'business asset' is one of the following:
- an asset used for the purposes of a trade carried on (alone or in partnership) by the taxpayer or, after 5 April 2004, any individual, trustee or personal representative; *or*
- an asset used for the purposes of a trade carried on by a 'qualifying company' (alone or, after 4 April 2004, in partnership); *or*
- shares or securities in a 'qualifying company'; *or*
- from 6 April 2000, an asset used for the purpose of any office or employment (full-time or part-time) held by the taxpayer with a person carrying on a trade; or
- before 6 April 2000, an asset held for the purposes of a qualifying office or employment to which the taxpayer is required to devote substantially the whole of his time.

Qualifying company. From 6 April 2000, a '*qualifying company*', by reference to an individual, is a trading company (or holding company of a trading group), where one or more of the following conditions is met:
- the company is unlisted (including an AIM company); *or*
- the taxpayer is an employee (full-time or part-time) of the company or a fellow group company (in which case the requirement that the company be a trading company etc is dropped, provided the taxpayer's interest in the company, including connected person holdings, is no more than 10%); *or*
- the taxpayer can exercise at least 5% of the voting rights.

Before 6 April 2000, a '*qualifying company*' is a trading company (or holding company of a trading group) in which the taxpayer holds shares entitling him to at least 5% of the voting rights where he is a full-time employee or 25% otherwise.

Leases

Depreciation table (TCGA 1992 Sch 8 para 1)

Yrs	%	Yrs	%	Yrs	%
50 (or more)	100	33	90·280	16	64·116
49	99·657	32	89·354	15	61·617
48	99·289	31	88·371	14	58·971
47	98·902	30	87·330	13	56·167
46	98·490	29	86·226	12	53·191
45	98·059	28	85·053	11	50·038
44	97·595	27	83·816	10	46·695
43	97·107	26	82·496	9	43·154
42	96·593	25	81·100	8	39·399
41	96·041	24	79·622	7	35·414
40	95·457	23	78·055	6	31·195
39	94·842	22	76·399	5	26·722
38	94·189	21	74·635	4	21·983
37	93·497	20	72·770	3	16·959
36	92·761	19	70·791	2	11·629
35	91·981	18	68·697	1	5·983
34	91·156	17	66·470	0	0

Formula: fraction of expenditure disallowed —

$$\frac{\text{Percentage for duration of lease at acquisition or expenditure} - \text{Percentage for duration of lease at disposal}}{\text{Percentage for duration of lease at acquisition or expenditure}}$$

Fractions of years:
Add one-twelfth of the difference between the percentage for the whole year and the next higher percentage for each additional month. Odd days under 14 are not counted; 14 odd days or more count as a month.

Short leases: premiums treated as rent (TA 1988 s 34, TCGA 1992 Sch 8 para 5; ITTOIA 2005 ss 277–281)
Part of premium for grant of a short lease which is chargeable to income tax as property income —
  $P - (2\% \times (n - 1) \times P)$
  Where P = amount of premium
  n = number of complete years which lease has to run when granted

Length of Lease (complete years)	Amount chargeable to CGT %	Income tax charge %	Length of Lease (complete years)	Amount chargeable to CGT %	Income tax charge %	Length of Lease (complete years)	Amount chargeable to CGT %	Income tax charge %
Over 50	100	0	34	66	34	17	32	68
50	98	2	33	64	36	16	30	70
49	96	4	32	62	38	15	28	72
48	94	6	31	60	40	14	26	74
47	92	8	30	58	42	13	24	76
46	90	10	29	56	44	12	22	78
45	88	12	28	54	46	11	20	80
44	86	14	27	52	48	10	18	82
43	84	16	26	50	50	9	16	84
42	82	18	25	48	52	8	14	86
41	80	20	24	46	54	7	12	88
40	78	22	23	44	56	6	10	90
39	76	24	22	42	58	5	8	92
38	74	26	21	40	60	4	6	94
37	72	28	20	38	62	3	4	96
36	70	30	19	36	64	2	2	98
35	68	32	18	34	66	1 or less	0	100

Reliefs

The following is a summary of the other main capital gains tax reliefs and exemptions.

Charities

Gains accruing to charities which are both applicable and applied for charitable purposes are exempt. The exemption was extended from 6 April 2002 to donations to Community Amateur Sports Clubs (CASCs)

Individuals

Compensation (injury to person, profession or vocation)	Exempt
Decorations for valour (acquired otherwise than for money or money's worth)	Gain exempt
Enterprise Investment Scheme (see p 59)	Gain on disposal after relevant three-year period exempt to extent full relief given on shares
Foreign currency acquired for personal expenditure	Gain exempt
Gifts for public benefit, works of art, historic buildings etc	No chargeable gain/allowable loss
Gilt-edged stock	No chargeable gain/allowable loss
Hold-over relief for gifts	Restricted to: (1) gifts of business assets (including unquoted shares in trading companies and holding companies of trading groups). Relief is not available on the transfer of shares or securities to a company made after 8 November 1999 (other than transfers between 6.4.03 and 20.10.03) (2) gifts of heritage property (3) gifts to heritage maintenance funds (4) gifts to political parties, and (5) gifts which are chargeable transfers for inheritance tax. Where available, transferee's acquisition cost treated as reduced by held-over gain.
Married persons or civil partners living together	No chargeable gain/allowable loss on transfers between spouses or civil partners
Motor vehicles	Gain exempt
Principal private residence	Gain exempt
If residence is partly let, exemption for the let part is limited to the smaller of—	(1) exemption on owner-occupied part and (2) £40,000
Qualifying corporate bonds	No chargeable gain (for loans made before 17 March 1998, allowable loss in certain cases if all or part of loss is irrecoverable)

Retirement relief (phased out from 6 April 1999 and no longer available for disposals after 5 April 2003)	Available for disposals (minimum age of retirement 50) after:
	5 April 2002 100% relief on gains up to £50,000
	                 50% relief on gains of £50,000.01–£200,000
	                 maximum relief of £125,000
	5 April 2001 100% relief on gains up to £100,000
	                 50% relief on gains of £100,000.01–£400,000
	                 maximum relief of £250,000
	5 April 2000 100% relief on gains up to £150,000
	                 50% relief on gains of £150,000.01–£600,000
	                 maximum relief of £375,000

Venture capital trusts (see p 59)	Gain on disposal of shares by original investor exempt if company still a venture capital trust. Exemption applies only to shares acquired up to the permitted maximum of £200,000 per year of assessment (£100,000 for shares acquired before 6 April 2004). Deferral relief is available on gains on assets where the disposal proceeds are reinvested in VCT shares issued before 6 April 2004 and within one year before or after the disposal. This relief is withdrawn for shares issued after that date.

Businesses
Roll-over relief for replacement of business assets

Qualifying assets:
    Buildings and land both occupied and used for the purposes of the trade
    Fixed plant and machinery
    Ships, aircraft and hovercraft
    Satellites, space stations and spacecraft
    Goodwill*
    Milk and potato quotas*
    Ewe and suckler cow premium quotas*
    Fish quotas (from 29 March 1999)*
    UK oil licences (from 1 July 1999)
    Payment entitlement under farmers' single payment scheme (from 22 March 2005)

The 'replacement' assets must be acquired within 12 months before or 3 years after the disposal of the old asset. Both assets must be within any of the above classes. Holdover relief is available where the new asset is a depreciating asset (having a predictable useful life not exceeding 60 years).

*From 1 April 2002 onwards, subject to transitional rules, these items are removed from the list for companies only (as they fall within the intangible assets regime from that date (FA 2002 Sch 29 para 132(5))).

Personal representatives
Allowable expenses

Expenses allowable for the costs of establishing title in computing chargeable gains on disposal of assets in a deceased person's estate: deaths occurring after 5 April 2004 (SP 2/04). (HMRC accepts computations based either on the scale or on the actual allowable expenditure incurred.)

Gross value of estate	Allowable expenditure
Up to £50,000	1.8% of the probate value of the assets sold by the personal representatives
Between £50,001 and £90,000	£900, to be divided between all the assets of the estate in proportion to the probate values and allowed in those proportions on assets sold by the personal representatives
Between £90,001 and £400,000	1% of the probate value of the assets sold
Between £400,001 and £500,000	£4,000, to be divided between all the assets of the estate in proportion to the probate values and allowed in those proportions on assets sold by the personal representatives
Between £500,001 and £1,000,000	0.8% of the probate value of the assets sold
Between £1,000,001 and £5,000,000	£8,000 to be divided between all the assets of the estate in proportion to the probate values and allowed in those proportions on assets sold by the personal representatives
Exceeding £5,000,000	0.16% of the probate value of the assets sold subject to a maximum of £10,000

Trustees
Allowable expenses

Expenses allowable in computing chargeable gains of corporate trustees in the administration of trusts and estates: acquisition, disposals and deemed disposals after 5 April 2004 (SP 2/04). (HMRC accepts computations based either on the scale or on the actual allowable expenditure incurred.)

Transfers of assets to beneficiaries etc	
(a) Quoted stocks and shares	
(i) One beneficiary	£25 per holding
(ii) More than one beneficiary	£25 per holding, divided equally between the beneficiaries
(b) Unquoted shares	As (a) above, plus any exceptional expenditure
(c) Other assets	As (a) above, plus any exceptional expenditure
Actual disposals and acquisitions	
(a) Quoted stocks and shares	Investment fee as charged by the trustees (where a comprehensive annual management fee is charged, the investment fee is taken to be £0.25 per £100 of the sale or purchase moneys)
(b) Unquoted shares	As (a) above, plus actual valuation costs
(c) Other assets	Investment fee (as (a) above), subject to a maximum of £75, plus actual valuation costs
Deemed disposals by trustees	
(a) Quoted stocks and shares	£8 per holding
(b) Unquoted shares	Actual valuation costs
(c) Other assets	Actual valuation costs

Indexation allowance – corporation tax on capital gains

For corporation tax purposes, an indexation allowance is given as a deduction in calculating gains on disposals from the amount realised (or deemed to be realised) on disposal. The indexation allowance is calculated by multiplying each item of allowable expenditure by:

$$\frac{RD - RI}{RI}$$

where RD = Retail prices index figure for month of disposal
RI = Retail prices index for month of expenditure (or March 1982 if later)

See page 25 for indexation allowances up to April 1998 and taper relief which applies thereafter on disposals made after 5 April 1998 by individuals, trustees and personal representatives. See page 42 for RPI values.

The factors below can be used to calculate the indexation allowance—

Month of disposal

		2003						2004										
	1982	July	Aug	Sept	Oct	Nov	Dec	Jan	Feb	Mar	Apr	May	June	July	Aug	Sept	Oct	Nov	Dec
B	Mar	1·282	1·286	1·297	1·299	1·300	1·310	1·305	1·314	1·324	1·338	1·348	1·351	1·351	1·359	1·368	1·374	1·379	1·390
a	Apr	1·237	1·241	1·252	1·253	1·254	1·264	1·259	1·268	1·278	1·291	1·301	1·305	1·305	1·312	1·321	1·327	1·332	1·343
s	May	1·221	1·225	1·236	1·237	1·238	1·248	1·243	1·252	1·262	1·275	1·285	1·289	1·289	1·296	1·305	1·311	1·316	1·327
e	June	1·215	1·219	1·230	1·231	1·232	1·242	1·237	1·246	1·255	1·269	1·279	1·282	1·282	1·290	1·298	1·304	1·309	1·320
	July	1·214	1·218	1·229	1·230	1·231	1·241	1·236	1·245	1·255	1·268	1·278	1·282	1·282	1·289	1·297	1·303	1·308	1·319
M	Aug	1·214	1·217	1·228	1·230	1·231	1·241	1·236	1·244	1·254	1·267	1·277	1·281	1·281	1·288	1·297	1·303	1·308	1·319
o	Sept	1·215	1·219	1·230	1·231	1·232	1·242	1·237	1·246	1·255	1·269	1·279	1·282	1·282	1·290	1·298	1·304	1·309	1·320
n	Oct	1·204	1·208	1·219	1·220	1·221	1·231	1·226	1·234	1·244	1·258	1·267	1·271	1·271	1·278	1·287	1·293	1·298	1·309
t	Nov	1·193	1·197	1·208	1·209	1·210	1·220	1·215	1·224	1·233	1·247	1·256	1·260	1·260	1·267	1·276	1·282	1·286	1·297
h	Dec	1·197	1·201	1·212	1·213	1·214	1·224	1·219	1·228	1·237	1·251	1·260	1·264	1·264	1·271	1·280	1·286	1·291	1·302
	1983																		
	Jan	1·195	1·198	1·209	1·210	1·212	1·221	1·216	1·225	1·235	1·248	1·258	1·261	1·261	1·268	1·277	1·283	1·288	1·299
	Feb	1·185	1·189	1·200	1·201	1·202	1·212	1·207	1·215	1·225	1·238	1·248	1·252	1·252	1·259	1·267	1·273	1·278	1·289
	Mar	1·181	1·185	1·196	1·197	1·198	1·208	1·203	1·211	1·221	1·234	1·244	1·247	1·247	1·255	1·263	1·269	1·274	1·285
	Apr	1·151	1·155	1·165	1·166	1·168	1·177	1·172	1·181	1·190	1·203	1·213	1·216	1·216	1·223	1·232	1·238	1·242	1·253
	May	1·142	1·146	1·156	1·157	1·159	1·168	1·163	1·172	1·181	1·194	1·203	1·207	1·207	1·214	1·222	1·228	1·233	1·244
	June	1·137	1·140	1·151	1·152	1·153	1·163	1·158	1·166	1·176	1·189	1·198	1·202	1·202	1·209	1·217	1·223	1·228	1·238
	July	1·125	1·129	1·140	1·141	1·142	1·151	1·147	1·155	1·164	1·177	1·186	1·190	1·190	1·197	1·205	1·211	1·216	1·226
	Aug	1·116	1·120	1·130	1·131	1·132	1·142	1·137	1·145	1·155	1·167	1·177	1·180	1·180	1·187	1·195	1·201	1·206	1·216
	Sept	1·107	1·110	1·121	1·122	1·123	1·132	1·128	1·136	1·145	1·158	1·167	1·171	1·171	1·178	1·186	1·192	1·196	1·207
	Oct	1·099	1·103	1·113	1·114	1·116	1·125	1·120	1·128	1·138	1·150	1·160	1·163	1·163	1·170	1·178	1·184	1·188	1·199
	Nov	1·092	1·095	1·106	1·107	1·108	1·117	1·113	1·121	1·130	1·143	1·152	1·155	1·155	1·162	1·170	1·176	1·181	1·191
	Dec	1·086	1·090	1·100	1·101	1·103	1·112	1·107	1·115	1·124	1·137	1·146	1·150	1·150	1·157	1·165	1·170	1·175	1·185
	1984																		
	Jan	1·088	1·091	1·101	1·103	1·104	1·113	1·108	1·116	1·126	1·138	1·148	1·151	1·151	1·158	1·166	1·172	1·176	1·187
	Feb	1·079	1·083	1·093	1·094	1·095	1·104	1·100	1·108	1·117	1·130	1·139	1·142	1·142	1·149	1·157	1·163	1·167	1·178
	Mar	1·073	1·076	1·086	1·087	1·089	1·098	1·093	1·101	1·110	1·123	1·132	1·135	1·135	1·142	1·150	1·156	1·161	1·171
	Apr	1·045	1·049	1·059	1·060	1·061	1·070	1·066	1·073	1·082	1·095	1·104	1·107	1·107	1·114	1·122	1·128	1·132	1·142
	May	1·038	1·041	1·051	1·052	1·053	1·062	1·058	1·060	1·075	1·087	1·096	1·100	1·100	1·106	1·114	1·120	1·124	1·134
	June	1·032	1·036	1·046	1·047	1·048	1·057	1·053	1·061	1·069	1·082	1·091	1·094	1·094	1·101	1·109	1·114	1·119	1·129
	July	1·035	1·038	1·048	1·049	1·051	1·059	1·055	1·063	1·072	1·084	1·093	1·097	1·097	1·103	1·111	1·117	1·121	1·131
	Aug	1·016	1·019	1·029	1·030	1·031	1·040	1·036	1·044	1·053	1·065	1·074	1·077	1·077	1·084	1·091	1·097	1·101	1·111
	Sept	1·012	1·015	1·025	1·026	1·027	1·036	1·032	1·040	1·049	1·061	1·070	1·073	1·073	1·080	1·087	1·093	1·097	1·107
	Oct	1·000	1·003	1·013	1·014	1·015	1·024	1·019	1·027	1·036	1·048	1·057	1·060	1·060	1·067	1·075	1·080	1·084	1·094
	Nov	·993	·997	1·007	1·008	1·009	1·018	1·013	1·021	1·030	1·042	1·051	1·054	1·054	1·060	1·068	1·074	1·078	1·088
	Dec	·995	·998	1·008	1·009	1·010	1·019	1·015	1·023	1·031	1·043	1·052	1·056	1·056	1·062	1·070	1·075	1·080	1·090
	1985																		
	Jan	·998	·991	1·001	1·002	1·003	1·012	1·008	1·015	1·024	1·036	1·045	1·048	1·048	1·055	1·062	1·068	1·072	1·082
	Feb	·972	·975	·985	·986	·987	·996	·992	·999	1·008	1·020	1·029	1·032	1·032	1·038	1·046	1·051	1·056	1·065
	Mar	·954	·957	·967	·968	·969	·977	·973	·981	·989	1·001	1·010	1·013	1·013	1·019	1·027	1·032	1·037	1·046
	Apr	·913	·916	·926	·927	·928	·936	·932	·939	·948	·959	·968	·971	·971	·977	·985	·990	·994	1·004
	May	·904	·907	·917	·918	·919	·927	·923	·930	·939	·950	·959	·962	·962	·968	·976	·981	·985	·995
	June	·900	·903	·913	·914	·915	·923	·919	·926	·935	·946	·955	·958	·958	·964	·971	·977	·981	·990
	July	·904	·907	·916	·917	·918	·927	·923	·930	·938	·950	·958	·961	·961	·968	·975	·980	·985	·994
	Aug	·899	·902	·911	·912	·913	·922	·918	·925	·933	·945	·953	·956	·956	·963	·970	·975	·979	·989
	Sept	·900	·903	·912	·913	·914	·923	·919	·926	·934	·946	·954	·957	·957	·964	·971	·976	·980	·990
	Oct	·897	·900	·909	·910	·911	·920	·915	·923	·931	·943	·951	·954	·954	·960	·968	·973	·977	·987
	Nov	·890	·893	·903	·904	·905	·913	·909	·916	·925	·936	·944	·947	·947	·954	·961	·966	·970	·980
	Dec	·888	·891	·900	·901	·902	·911	·906	·914	·922	·933	·942	·945	·945	·951	·958	·964	·968	·977

Month of disposal

		2005												2006					
	1982	Jan	Feb	Mar	Apr	May	June	July	Aug	Sept	Oct	Nov	Dec	Jan	Feb	Mar	Apr	May	June
B	Mar	1·378	1·387	1·398	1·412	1·417	1·419	1·419	1·424	1·431	1·433	1·437	1·443	1·434	1·445	1·455	1·473	1·489	1·499
a	Apr	1·331	1·340	1·351	1·364	1·369	1·372	1·372	1·377	1·383	1·385	1·389	1·395	1·386	1·396	1·406	1·425	1·440	1·449
s	May	1·314	1·323	1·334	1·347	1·352	1·355	1·355	1·360	1·366	1·368	1·372	1·378	1·369	1·379	1·389	1·407	1·422	1·432
e	Jun	1·308	1·316	1·327	1·341	1·346	1·348	1·348	1·353	1·359	1·362	1·365	1·371	1·363	1·373	1·382	1·401	1·415	1·425
	Jul	1·307	1·316	1·327	1·340	1·345	1·347	1·347	1·352	1·358	1·361	1·365	1·371	1·362	1·372	1·382	1·400	1·415	1·424
M	Aug	1·306	1·315	1·326	1·339	1·344	1·347	1·347	1·352	1·358	1·360	1·364	1·370	1·361	1·371	1·381	1·399	1·414	1·424
o	Sep	1·308	1·316	1·327	1·341	1·346	1·348	1·348	1·353	1·359	1·362	1·365	1·371	1·363	1·373	1·382	1·401	1·415	1·425
n	Oct	1·296	1·305	1·316	1·329	1·334	1·337	1·337	1·341	1·348	1·350	1·354	1·360	1·351	1·361	1·371	1·389	1·403	1·413
t	Nov	1·285	1·294	1·305	1·318	1·323	1·325	1·325	1·330	1·336	1·338	1·342	1·348	1·340	1·349	1·359	1·377	1·392	1·401
h	Dec	1·289	1·298	1·309	1·322	1·327	1·329	1·329	1·334	1·340	1·343	1·346	1·352	1·344	1·354	1·363	1·382	1·396	1·406
	1983																		
	Jan	1·287	1·295	1·306	1·319	1·324	1·327	1·327	1·331	1·337	1·340	1·344	1·350	1·341	1·351	1·360	1·379	1·393	1·403
	Feb	1·277	1·285	1·296	1·309	1·314	1·317	1·317	1·321	1·327	1·330	1·333	1·340	1·331	1·341	1·350	1·368	1·383	1·393
	Mar	1·273	1·281	1·292	1·305	1·310	1·312	1·312	1·317	1·323	1·326	1·329	1·335	1·327	1·336	1·346	1·364	1·379	1·388
	Apr	1·241	1·250	1·260	1·273	1·278	1·280	1·280	1·285	1·291	1·293	1·297	1·303	1·295	1·304	1·314	1·331	1·346	1·355
	May	1·232	1·240	1·251	1·264	1·268	1·271	1·271	1·276	1·281	1·284	1·287	1·293	1·285	1·294	1·304	1·322	1·336	1·345
	Jun	1·227	1·235	1·245	1·258	1·263	1·265	1·265	1·270	1·276	1·278	1·282	1·288	1·280	1·289	1·298	1·316	1·330	1·340
	Jul	1·215	1·223	1·233	1·246	1·251	1·253	1·253	1·258	1·264	1·266	1·270	1·276	1·267	1·277	1·286	1·304	1·318	1·327
	Aug	1·205	1·213	1·223	1·236	1·241	1·243	1·243	1·248	1·254	1·256	1·260	1·265	1·257	1·267	1·276	1·293	1·307	1·317
	Sep	1·195	1·203	1·214	1·226	1·231	1·233	1·233	1·238	1·244	1·246	1·250	1·255	1·247	1·257	1·266	1·283	1·297	1·307
	Oct	1·187	1·195	1·206	1·219	1·223	1·226	1·226	1·230	1·236	1·238	1·242	1·248	1·239	1·249	1·258	1·275	1·289	1·298
	Nov	1·180	1·188	1·198	1·211	1·215	1·218	1·218	1·222	1·228	1·230	1·234	1·240	1·232	1·241	1·250	1·267	1·281	1·290
	Dec	1·174	1·182	1·192	1·205	1·210	1·212	1·212	1·216	1·222	1·225	1·228	1·234	1·226	1·235	1·244	1·261	1·275	1·284
	1984																		
	Jan	1·175	1·183	1·194	1·206	1·211	1·213	1·213	1·218	1·224	1·226	1·229	1·235	1·227	1·236	1·245	1·263	1·276	1·286
	Feb	1·166	1·174	1·185	1·197	1·202	1·204	1·204	1·209	1·214	1·217	1·220	1·226	1·218	1·227	1·236	1·253	1·267	1·276
	Mar	1·159	1·167	1·178	1·190	1·195	1·197	1·197	1·202	1·207	1·210	1·213	1·219	1·211	1·220	1·229	1·246	1·260	1·269
	Apr	1·131	1·139	1·149	1·161	1·166	1·168	1·168	1·173	1·178	1·181	1·184	1·190	1·182	1·191	1·200	1·217	1·230	1·239
	May	1·123	1·131	1·141	1·153	1·158	1·160	1·160	1·165	1·170	1·173	1·176	1·182	1·174	1·183	1·192	1·209	1·222	1·231
	Jun	1·118	1·126	1·136	1·148	1·152	1·155	1·155	1·159	1·165	1·167	1·170	1·176	1·168	1·177	1·186	1·203	1·216	1·225
	Jul	1·120	1·128	1·138	1·150	1·155	1·157	1·157	1·162	1·167	1·169	1·173	1·178	1·171	1·180	1·189	1·205	1·219	1·228
	Aug	1·100	1·108	1·118	1·130	1·135	1·137	1·137	1·142	1·147	1·149	1·153	1·158	1·150	1·159	1·168	1·185	1·198	1·207
	Sep	1·096	1·104	1·114	1·126	1·131	1·133	1·133	1·137	1·143	1·145	1·148	1·154	1·146	1·155	1·164	1·181	1·194	1·203
	Oct	1·083	1·091	1·101	1·113	1·118	1·120	1·120	1·124	1·130	1·132	1·135	1·141	1·133	1·142	1·151	1·167	1·180	1·189
	Nov	1·077	1·085	1·095	1·107	1·111	1·113	1·113	1·118	1·123	1·125	1·129	1·134	1·126	1·135	1·144	1·161	1·174	1·183
	Dec	1·079	1·086	1·096	1·108	1·113	1·115	1·115	1·119	1·125	1·127	1·130	1·136	1·128	1·137	1·146	1·162	1·176	1·184
	1985																		
	Jan	1·071	1·079	1·089	1·101	1·105	1·107	1·107	1·112	1·117	1·119	1·123	1·128	1·121	1·129	1·138	1·155	1·168	1·176
	Feb	1·055	1·062	1·072	1·084	1·088	1·091	1·091	1·095	1·100	1·102	1·106	1·111	1·104	1·112	1·121	1·137	1·150	1·159
	Mar	1·036	1·043	1·053	1·065	1·069	1·071	1·071	1·075	1·081	1·083	1·086	1·092	1·084	1·093	1·101	1·117	1·130	1·139
	Apr	·993	1·000	1·010	1·022	1·026	1·028	1·028	1·032	1·037	1·039	1·043	1·048	1·041	1·049	1·057	1·073	1·086	1·094
	May	·984	·991	1·001	1·012	1·017	1·019	1·019	1·023	1·028	1·030	1·033	1·039	1·031	1·040	1·048	1·064	1·076	1·085
	Jun	·980	·987	·997	1·008	1·012	1·014	1·014	1·019	1·024	1·026	1·029	1·034	1·027	1·035	1·044	1·059	1·072	1·080
	Jul	·984	·991	1·000	1·012	1·016	1·018	1·018	1·022	1·028	1·030	1·033	1·038	1·031	1·039	1·048	1·063	1·076	1·084
	Aug	·978	·986	·995	1·007	1·011	1·013	1·013	1·017	1·022	1·024	1·027	1·033	1·025	1·034	1·042	1·058	1·070	1·079
	Sep	·979	·987	·996	1·008	1·012	1·014	1·014	1·018	1·023	1·025	1·029	1·034	1·026	1·035	1·043	1·059	1·072	1·080
	Oct	·976	·983	·993	1·004	1·009	1·011	1·011	1·015	1·020	1·022	1·025	1·031	1·023	1·032	1·040	1·056	1·068	1·077
	Nov	·969	·977	·986	·998	1·002	1·004	1·004	1·008	1·013	1·015	1·018	1·024	1·016	1·025	1·033	1·049	1·061	1·069
	Dec	·967	·974	·983	·995	·999	1·001	1·001	1·005	1·011	1·013	1·016	1·021	1·014	1·022	1·030	1·046	1·058	1·067

Indexation allowance — continued

Month of disposal

		2003						2004									
	1986	July	Aug	Sept	Oct	Nov	Dec	Jan	Feb	Mar	Apr	May	June	July	Aug	Sept	Oct	Nov	Dec
	Jan	·884	·887	·896	·897	·898	·907	·902	·910	·918	·929	·938	·941	·941	·947	·954	·960	·964	·973
	Feb	·877	·880	·889	·890	·891	·900	·895	·903	·911	·922	·931	·934	·934	·940	·947	·952	·956	·966
	Mar	·874	·877	·887	·888	·889	·897	·893	·900	·908	·920	·928	·931	·931	·937	·945	·950	·954	·963
	Apr	·856	·859	·869	·870	·871	·879	·875	·882	·890	·901	·910	·913	·913	·919	·926	·931	·935	·944
	May	·853	·856	·865	·866	·867	·875	·871	·878	·887	·898	·906	·909	·909	·915	·922	·928	·932	·941
	June	·854	·857	·866	·867	·868	·876	·872	·879	·888	·899	·907	·910	·910	·916	·923	·929	·933	·942
	July	·859	·862	·871	·873	·874	·882	·878	·885	·893	·904	·913	·916	·916	·922	·929	·934	·938	·947
	Aug	·853	·856	·866	·867	·868	·876	·872	·879	·887	·898	·907	·910	·910	·916	·923	·928	·932	·941
	Sept	·844	·847	·857	·858	·859	·867	·863	·870	·878	·889	·897	·900	·900	·906	·913	·919	·923	·932
	Oct	·841	·845	·854	·855	·856	·864	·860	·867	·875	·886	·894	·897	·897	·903	·911	·916	·920	·929
	Nov	·826	·829	·838	·839	·840	·848	·844	·851	·859	·870	·878	·881	·881	·887	·894	·899	·904	·913
	Dec	·820	·823	·832	·833	·834	·842	·838	·845	·853	·864	·872	·875	·875	·881	·888	·893	·897	·906
	1987																		
	Jan	·813	·816	·825	·826	·827	·835	·831	·838	·846	·857	·865	·868	·868	·874	·881	·886	·890	·899
	Feb	·806	·809	·818	·819	·820	·828	·824	·831	·839	·850	·858	·861	·861	·867	·874	·878	·882	·891
	Mar	·802	·805	·814	·815	·816	·824	·820	·827	·835	·846	·854	·857	·857	·863	·870	·875	·879	·888
	Apr	·781	·784	·793	·794	·795	·803	·799	·806	·813	·824	·832	·835	·835	·841	·848	·853	·857	·865
	May	·779	·782	·791	·792	·793	·801	·797	·804	·812	·822	·830	·833	·833	·839	·846	·851	·855	·864
	June	·779	·782	·791	·792	·793	·801	·797	·804	·812	·822	·830	·833	·833	·839	·846	·851	·855	·864
	July	·781	·784	·793	·794	·795	·803	·799	·806	·813	·824	·832	·835	·835	·841	·848	·853	·857	·865
	Aug	·776	·779	·787	·788	·789	·797	·793	·800	·808	·819	·827	·830	·830	·835	·842	·847	·851	·860
	Sept	·771	·773	·782	·783	·784	·792	·788	·795	·803	·813	·821	·824	·824	·830	·837	·842	·846	·854
	Oct	·762	·765	·774	·775	·776	·783	·779	·786	·794	·805	·812	·815	·815	·821	·828	·833	·837	·845
	Nov	·753	·756	·765	·766	·767	·775	·771	·778	·785	·796	·804	·807	·807	·812	·819	·824	·828	·837
	Dec	·755	·758	·767	·768	·769	·776	·773	·779	·787	·798	·805	·808	·808	·814	·821	·826	·830	·838
	1988																		
	Jan	·755	·758	·767	·768	·769	·776	·773	·779	·787	·798	·805	·808	·808	·814	·821	·826	·830	·838
	Feb	·748	·751	·760	·761	·762	·770	·766	·772	·780	·791	·798	·801	·801	·807	·814	·819	·823	·831
	Mar	·742	·744	·753	·754	·755	·763	·759	·766	·773	·784	·792	·794	·794	·800	·807	·812	·816	·824
	Apr	·714	·716	·725	·726	·727	·734	·731	·737	·745	·755	·763	·766	·766	·771	·778	·783	·786	·795
	May	·707	·710	·718	·719	·720	·728	·724	·731	·738	·749	·756	·759	·759	·765	·771	·776	·780	·788
	June	·701	·704	·712	·713	·714	·721	·718	·724	·732	·742	·750	·752	·752	·758	·765	·769	·773	·781
	July	·699	·702	·710	·711	·712	·720	·716	·723	·730	·740	·748	·751	·751	·756	·763	·768	·771	·780
	Aug	·680	·683	·691	·692	·693	·701	·697	·703	·711	·721	·728	·731	·731	·737	·743	·748	·752	·760
	Sept	·673	·675	·684	·685	·685	·693	·689	·696	·703	·713	·720	·723	·723	·729	·735	·740	·744	·752
	Oct	·656	·658	·667	·668	·668	·676	·672	·679	·686	·696	·703	·706	·706	·711	·718	·722	·726	·734
	Nov	·648	·651	·659	·660	·661	·668	·665	·671	·678	·688	·695	·698	·698	·704	·710	·715	·718	·726
	Dec	·644	·646	·655	·655	·656	·664	·660	·666	·674	·684	·691	·694	·694	·699	·705	·710	·714	·722
	1989																		
	Jan	·633	·636	·644	·645	·646	·653	·650	·656	·663	·673	·680	·683	·683	·688	·695	·699	·703	·711
	Feb	·622	·624	·632	·633	·634	·641	·638	·644	·651	·661	·668	·671	·671	·676	·682	·687	·691	·699
	Mar	·614	·617	·625	·626	·627	·634	·630	·637	·644	·654	·661	·663	·663	·669	·675	·679	·683	·691
	Apr	·586	·589	·597	·598	·598	·605	·602	·608	·615	·625	·632	·634	·634	·640	·646	·650	·654	·661
	May	·577	·579	·587	·588	·589	·596	·592	·598	·605	·615	·622	·624	·624	·630	·636	·640	·643	·651
	June	·571	·574	·581	·582	·583	·590	·587	·593	·600	·609	·616	·619	·619	·624	·630	·634	·638	·646
	July	·570	·572	·580	·581	·582	·589	·585	·591	·598	·608	·615	·617	·617	·623	·629	·633	·636	·644
	Aug	·566	·568	·576	·577	·578	·585	·581	·587	·594	·604	·611	·613	·613	·618	·624	·629	·632	·640
	Sept	·555	·557	·565	·566	·567	·574	·570	·576	·583	·593	·599	·602	·602	·607	·613	·617	·621	·629
	Oct	·543	·546	·553	·554	·555	·562	·558	·564	·571	·580	·587	·590	·590	·595	·601	·605	·609	·616
	Nov	·530	·532	·540	·541	·542	·549	·545	·551	·558	·567	·574	·576	·576	·581	·587	·592	·595	·603
	Dec	·526	·529	·536	·537	·538	·545	·541	·547	·554	·563	·570	·572	·572	·577	·583	·588	·591	·598

B a s e M o n t h

Month of disposal

		2005												2006					
	1986	Jan	Feb	Mar	Apr	May	June	July	Aug	Sept	Oct	Nov	Dec	Jan	Feb	Mar	Apr	May	June
B	Jan	·963	·970	·979	·991	·995	·997	·997	1·001	1·006	1·008	1·011	1·017	1·009	1·018	1·026	1·042	1·054	1·062
a	Feb	·955	·963	·972	·983	·988	·990	·990	·994	·999	1·001	1·004	1·009	1·002	1·010	1·019	1·034	1·047	1·055
s	Mar	·953	·960	·969	·981	·985	·987	·987	·991	·996	·998	1·001	1·007	·999	1·008	1·016	1·031	1·044	1·052
e	Apr	·934	·941	·950	·962	·966	·968	·968	·972	·977	·979	·982	·987	·980	·988	·997	1·012	1·024	1·032
	May	·931	·938	·947	·958	·962	·964	·964	·968	·974	·976	·979	·984	·977	·985	·993	1·008	1·021	1·029
M	Jun	·932	·939	·948	·959	·963	·965	·965	·969	·975	·977	·980	·985	·978	·986	·994	1·009	1·022	1·030
o	Jul	·937	·944	·954	·965	·969	·971	·971	·975	·980	·982	·985	·990	·983	·991	1·000	1·015	1·027	1·036
n	Aug	·931	·938	·947	·959	·963	·965	·965	·969	·974	·976	·979	·984	·977	·985	·993	1·009	1·021	1·029
t	Sep	·922	·929	·938	·949	·953	·955	·955	·959	·964	·966	·969	·975	·967	·976	·984	·999	1·011	1·019
h	Oct	·919	·926	·935	·946	·950	·952	·952	·956	·961	·963	·966	·971	·964	·973	·981	·996	1·008	1·016
	Nov	·903	·910	·919	·930	·934	·936	·936	·940	·945	·947	·950	·955	·948	·956	·964	·979	·991	·999
	Dec	·896	·903	·912	·923	·927	·929	·929	·933	·938	·940	·943	·948	·941	·949	·957	·973	·985	·993
	1987																		
	Jan	·889	·896	·905	·916	·920	·922	·922	·926	·931	·933	·936	·941	·934	·942	·950	·965	·977	·985
	Feb	·881	·888	·897	·908	·912	·914	·914	·918	·923	·925	·928	·933	·926	·934	·942	·957	·969	·977
	Mar	·878	·885	·894	·905	·909	·911	·911	·915	·919	·921	·924	·929	·922	·930	·938	·953	·965	·973
	Apr	·856	·862	·871	·882	·886	·888	·888	·892	·897	·899	·902	·907	·900	·908	·916	·930	·942	·950
	May	·854	·861	·869	·880	·884	·886	·886	·890	·895	·897	·900	·905	·898	·906	·914	·928	·940	·948
	Jun	·854	·861	·869	·880	·884	·886	·886	·890	·895	·897	·900	·905	·898	·906	·914	·928	·940	·948
	Jul	·856	·862	·871	·882	·886	·888	·888	·892	·897	·899	·902	·907	·900	·908	·916	·930	·942	·950
	Aug	·850	·857	·866	·877	·881	·882	·882	·886	·891	·893	·896	·901	·894	·902	·910	·925	·936	·944
	Sep	·845	·852	·860	·871	·875	·877	·877	·881	·886	·888	·891	·896	·889	·896	·904	·919	·931	·938
	Oct	·836	·843	·851	·862	·866	·868	·868	·872	·877	·879	·881	·886	·879	·887	·895	·910	·921	·929
	Nov	·827	·834	·842	·853	·857	·859	·859	·863	·868	·869	·872	·877	·870	·878	·886	·900	·912	·920
	Dec	·829	·835	·844	·855	·859	·861	·861	·864	·869	·871	·874	·879	·872	·880	·888	·902	·914	·922
	1988																		
	Jan	·829	·835	·844	·855	·859	·861	·861	·864	·869	·871	·874	·879	·872	·880	·888	·902	·914	·922
	Feb	·822	·828	·837	·848	·851	·853	·853	·857	·862	·864	·867	·872	·865	·873	·880	·895	·906	·914
	Mar	·815	·821	·830	·841	·844	·846	·846	·850	·855	·857	·860	·865	·858	·866	·873	·888	·899	·907
	Apr	·785	·792	·801	·811	·815	·817	·817	·820	·825	·827	·830	·835	·828	·836	·843	·857	·869	·876
	May	·779	·785	·794	·804	·808	·810	·810	·814	·818	·820	·823	·828	·821	·829	·836	·850	·862	·869
	Jun	·772	·779	·787	·797	·801	·803	·803	·807	·811	·813	·816	·821	·814	·822	·829	·843	·855	·862
	Jul	·770	·777	·785	·796	·799	·801	·801	·805	·810	·812	·814	·819	·813	·820	·828	·842	·853	·860
	Aug	·751	·757	·766	·776	·779	·781	·781	·785	·790	·791	·794	·799	·792	·800	·807	·821	·832	·840
	Sep	·743	·749	·757	·768	·771	·773	·773	·777	·781	·783	·786	·791	·784	·792	·799	·813	·824	·831
	Oct	·725	·732	·740	·750	·753	·755	·755	·759	·763	·765	·768	·773	·766	·774	·781	·795	·805	·813
	Nov	·717	·724	·732	·742	·745	·747	·747	·751	·755	·757	·760	·765	·758	·765	·773	·786	·797	·805
	Dec	·713	·719	·727	·737	·741	·743	·743	·746	·751	·752	·755	·760	·753	·761	·768	·782	·792	·800
	1989																		
	Jan	·702	·708	·716	·726	·730	·732	·732	·735	·740	·741	·744	·749	·742	·750	·757	·770	·781	·788
	Feb	·690	·696	·704	·714	·717	·719	·719	·723	·727	·729	·732	·736	·730	·737	·744	·758	·768	·775
	Mar	·682	·688	·696	·706	·710	·711	·711	·715	·720	·721	·724	·728	·722	·729	·736	·750	·760	·768
	Apr	·653	·659	·667	·676	·680	·682	·682	·685	·689	·691	·694	·698	·692	·699	·706	·719	·730	·737
	May	·643	·649	·657	·666	·670	·671	·671	·675	·679	·681	·683	·688	·682	·689	·696	·709	·719	·726
	Jun	·637	·643	·651	·660	·664	·666	·666	·669	·673	·675	·678	·682	·676	·683	·690	·703	·713	·720
	Jul	·635	·642	·649	·659	·662	·664	·664	·668	·672	·674	·676	·681	·674	·681	·688	·701	·712	·719
	Aug	·631	·637	·645	·655	·658	·660	·660	·663	·668	·669	·672	·676	·670	·677	·684	·697	·707	·714
	Sep	·620	·626	·634	·643	·647	·648	·648	·652	·656	·658	·660	·665	·659	·666	·672	·685	·696	·702
	Oct	·608	·614	·621	·631	·634	·636	·636	·639	·643	·645	·648	·652	·646	·653	·660	·672	·683	·689
	Nov	·594	·600	·608	·617	·620	·622	·622	·625	·630	·631	·634	·638	·632	·639	·646	·658	·668	·675
	Dec	·590	·596	·604	·613	·616	·618	·618	·621	·625	·627	·630	·634	·628	·635	·641	·654	·664	·671

33

Indexation allowance — continued

Month of disposal

Base Month		2003						2004										
		July	Aug	Sept	Oct	Nov	Dec	Jan	Feb	Mar	Apr	May	June	July	Aug	Sept	Oct	Nov	Dec
1990	Jan	·517	·520	·527	·528	·529	·536	·532	·538	·545	·554	·561	·563	·563	·568	·574	·578	·582	·589
	Feb	·508	·511	·518	·519	·520	·527	·523	·529	·536	·545	·552	·554	·554	·559	·565	·569	·572	·580
	Mar	·493	·496	·503	·504	·505	·512	·508	·514	·521	·530	·536	·539	·539	·544	·549	·554	·557	·564
	Apr	·449	·452	·459	·460	·460	·467	·464	·469	·476	·484	·491	·493	·493	·498	·504	·508	·511	·518
	May	·437	·439	·446	·447	·448	·454	·451	·456	·463	·471	·478	·480	·480	·485	·490	·494	·498	·505
	June	·431	·433	·440	·441	·442	·448	·445	·451	·457	·466	·472	·474	·474	·479	·485	·489	·492	·499
	July	·430	·432	·439	·440	·441	·447	·444	·450	·456	·465	·471	·473	·473	·478	·483	·487	·491	·498
	Aug	·415	·418	·425	·425	·426	·432	·429	·435	·441	·450	·456	·458	·458	·463	·468	·472	·475	·482
	Sept	·402	·404	·411	·412	·413	·419	·416	·422	·428	·436	·442	·445	·445	·449	·455	·459	·462	·469
	Oct	·391	·394	·401	·401	·402	·408	·405	·411	·417	·425	·431	·434	·434	·438	·444	·447	·450	·457
	Nov	·395	·397	·404	·405	·405	·412	·408	·414	·420	·428	·435	·437	·437	·442	·447	·451	·454	·461
	Dec	·396	·398	·405	·406	·406	·413	·410	·415	·421	·430	·436	·438	·438	·443	·448	·452	·455	·462
1991	Jan	·392	·395	·402	·402	·403	·409	·406	·412	·418	·426	·432	·435	·435	·439	·445	·449	·452	·459
	Feb	·385	·387	·394	·395	·396	·402	·399	·404	·410	·419	·425	·427	·427	·432	·437	·441	·444	·451
	Mar	·380	·382	·389	·390	·390	·396	·393	·399	·405	·413	·419	·422	·422	·426	·432	·435	·438	·445
	Apr	·362	·364	·371	·372	·373	·379	·376	·381	·387	·395	·401	·403	·403	·408	·413	·417	·420	·427
	May	·358	·360	·367	·368	·369	·375	·372	·377	·383	·391	·397	·399	·399	·404	·409	·413	·416	·422
	June	·352	·354	·361	·362	·362	·368	·365	·371	·377	·385	·391	·393	·393	·397	·403	·406	·409	·416
	July	·355	·357	·364	·365	·365	·371	·368	·374	·380	·388	·394	·396	·396	·401	·406	·410	·413	·419
	Aug	·352	·354	·361	·362	·362	·368	·365	·371	·377	·385	·391	·393	·393	·397	·403	·406	·409	·416
	Sept	·347	·349	·356	·357	·357	·363	·360	·366	·371	·380	·386	·388	·388	·392	·397	·401	·404	·411
	Oct	·342	·344	·351	·352	·352	·358	·355	·360	·366	·375	·380	·383	·383	·387	·392	·396	·399	·406
	Nov	·337	·339	·346	·347	·347	·353	·350	·355	·361	·369	·375	·378	·378	·382	·387	·391	·394	·400
	Dec	·336	·338	·345	·346	·346	·352	·349	·354	·360	·368	·374	·377	·377	·381	·386	·390	·393	·399
1992	Jan	·337	·339	·346	·347	·347	·353	·350	·355	·361	·369	·375	·378	·378	·382	·387	·391	·394	·400
	Feb	·330	·332	·339	·340	·340	·346	·343	·348	·354	·362	·368	·371	·371	·375	·380	·384	·387	·393
	Mar	·326	·328	·335	·336	·337	·342	·339	·345	·350	·358	·364	·366	·366	·371	·376	·380	·383	·389
	Apr	·306	·308	·315	·316	·316	·322	·319	·324	·330	·338	·344	·346	·346	·350	·355	·359	·362	·368
	May	·302	·304	·310	·311	·312	·317	·314	·319	·325	·333	·339	·341	·341	·345	·350	·354	·357	·363
	June	·302	·304	·310	·311	·312	·317	·314	·319	·325	·333	·339	·341	·341	·345	·350	·354	·357	·363
	July	·306	·308	·315	·316	·316	·322	·319	·324	·330	·338	·344	·346	·346	·350	·355	·359	·362	·368
	Aug	·305	·307	·314	·315	·315	·321	·318	·323	·329	·337	·343	·345	·345	·349	·354	·358	·361	·367
	Sept	·301	·303	·309	·310	·311	·316	·313	·319	·324	·332	·338	·340	·340	·344	·349	·353	·356	·362
	Oct	·296	·298	·305	·305	·306	·312	·309	·314	·320	·327	·333	·335	·335	·340	·345	·348	·351	·357
	Nov	·298	·300	·306	·307	·308	·314	·311	·316	·321	·329	·335	·337	·337	·341	·346	·350	·353	·359
	Dec	·302	·305	·311	·312	·313	·318	·315	·320	·326	·334	340	·342	·342	·346	·351	·355	·358	·364
1993	Jan	·315	·317	·323	·324	·325	·331	·328	·333	·339	·347	·352	·355	·355	·359	·364	·368	·371	·377
	Feb	·306	·308	·315	·316	·316	·322	·319	·324	·330	·338	·344	·346	·346	·350	·355	·359	·362	·368
	Mar	·302	·304	·310	·311	·312	·317	·314	·319	·325	·333	·339	·341	·341	·345	·350	·354	·357	·363
	Apr	·289	·292	·298	·299	·299	·305	·302	·307	·313	·321	·326	·329	·329	·333	·338	·341	·344	·351
	May	·285	·287	·293	·294	·295	·300	·298	·303	·308	·316	·322	·324	·324	·328	·333	·337	·339	·346
	June	·286	·288	·294	·295	·296	·301	·299	·304	·309	·317	·323	·325	·325	·329	·334	·338	·340	·347
	July	·289	·291	·297	·298	·299	·304	·301	·306	·312	·320	·326	·328	·328	·332	·337	·340	·343	·350
	Aug	·283	·285	·292	·292	·293	·299	·296	·301	·306	·314	·320	·322	·322	·326	·331	·335	·338	·344
	Sept	·278	·280	·286	·287	·288	·293	·290	·295	·301	·309	·314	·316	·316	·321	·326	·329	·332	·338
	Oct	·279	·281	·287	·288	·288	·294	·291	·296	·302	·310	·315	·317	·317	·322	·327	·330	·333	·339
	Nov	·280	·282	·289	·290	·290	·296	·293	·298	·304	·311	·317	·319	·319	·323	·328	·332	·335	·341
	Dec	·278	·280	·286	·287	·288	·293	·290	·295	·301	·309	·314	·316	·316	·321	·326	·329	·332	·338

Month of disposal

Base Month		2005												2006					
	1990	Jan	Feb	Mar	Apr	May	June	July	Aug	Sept	Oct	Nov	Dec	Jan	Feb	Mar	Apr	May	June
	Jan	·581	·587	·594	·603	·607	·608	·608	·612	·616	·618	·620	·624	·618	·625	·632	·644	·654	·661
	Feb	·572	·577	·585	·594	·597	·599	·599	·602	·606	·608	·611	·615	·609	·616	·622	·635	·645	·651
	Mar	·556	·562	·569	·578	·582	·583	·583	·586	·591	·592	·595	·599	·593	·600	·606	·619	·629	·635
	Apr	·510	·516	·523	·532	·535	·536	·536	·540	·544	·545	·548	·552	·546	·552	·559	·571	·580	·587
	May	·497	·502	·510	·518	·521	·523	·523	·526	·530	·532	·534	·538	·532	·539	·545	·557	·567	·573
	Jun	·491	·496	·504	·512	·515	·517	·517	·520	·524	·526	·528	·532	·526	·533	·539	·551	·560	·567
	Jul	·490	·495	·502	·511	·514	·516	·516	·519	·523	·524	·527	·531	·525	·532	·538	·550	·559	·565
	Aug	·475	·480	·487	·496	·499	·500	·500	·504	·507	·509	·511	·515	·510	·516	·522	·534	·543	·550
	Sep	·461	·466	·473	·482	·485	·486	·486	·490	·493	·495	·497	·501	·496	·502	·508	·520	·529	·535
	Oct	·450	·455	·462	·470	·474	·475	·475	·478	·482	·483	·486	·490	·484	·490	·497	·508	·517	·523
	Nov	·453	·458	·465	·474	·477	·478	·478	·482	·485	·487	·489	·493	·488	·494	·500	·512	·521	·527
	Dec	·454	·460	·467	·475	·478	·480	·480	·483	·487	·488	·490	·494	·489	·495	·501	·513	·522	·528
	1991																		
	Jan	·451	·456	·463	·472	·475	·476	·476	·479	·483	·485	·487	·491	·485	·492	·498	·509	·518	·525
	Feb	·443	·448	·455	·464	·467	·468	·468	·471	·475	·477	·479	·483	·477	·484	·490	·501	·510	·516
	Mar	·438	·443	·450	·458	·461	·463	·463	·466	·470	·471	·473	·477	·472	·478	·484	·495	·505	·511
	Apr	·419	·424	·431	·440	·443	·444	·444	·447	·451	·452	·455	·458	·453	·459	·465	·476	·485	·491
	May	·415	·420	·427	·435	·438	·440	·440	·443	·446	·448	·450	·454	·449	·455	·461	·472	·481	·487
	Jun	·409	·414	·421	·429	·432	·433	·433	·436	·440	·441	·444	·447	·442	·448	·454	·465	·474	·480
	Jul	·412	·417	·424	·432	·435	·436	·436	·439	·443	·445	·447	·451	·445	·451	·457	·469	·478	·484
	Aug	·409	·414	·421	·429	·432	·433	·433	·436	·440	·441	·444	·447	·442	·448	·454	·465	·474	·480
	Sep	·403	·409	·415	·423	·426	·428	·428	·431	·435	·436	·438	·442	·437	·443	·449	·460	·469	·475
	Oct	·398	·403	·410	·418	·421	·423	·423	·426	·429	·431	·433	·437	·432	·437	·443	·454	·463	·469
	Nov	·393	·398	·405	·413	·416	·417	·417	·420	·424	·426	·428	·431	·426	·432	·438	·449	·458	·464
	Dec	·392	·397	·404	·412	·415	·416	·416	·419	·423	·424	·427	·430	·425	·431	·437	·448	·457	·463
	1992																		
	Jan	·393	·398	·405	·413	·416	·417	·417	·420	·424	·426	·428	·431	·426	·432	·438	·449	·458	·464
	Feb	·386	·391	·398	·406	·409	·410	·410	·413	·417	·418	·420	·424	·419	·425	·431	·442	·450	·456
	Mar	·382	·387	·394	·402	·405	·406	·406	·409	·413	·414	·416	·420	·415	·421	·426	·437	·446	·452
	Apr	·361	·366	·372	·380	·383	·385	·385	·388	·391	·393	·395	·398	·393	·399	·405	·416	·424	·430
	May	·356	·361	·368	·375	·378	·380	·380	·383	·386	·388	·390	·393	·388	·394	·400	·411	·419	·425
	Jun	·356	·361	·368	·375	·378	·380	·380	·383	·386	·388	·390	·393	·388	·394	·400	·411	·419	·425
	Jul	·361	·366	·372	·380	·383	·385	·385	·388	·391	·393	·395	·398	·393	·399	·405	·416	·424	·430
	Aug	·360	·365	·371	·379	·382	·384	·384	·387	·390	·392	·394	·397	·392	·398	·404	·415	·423	·429
	Sep	·355	·360	·367	·374	·377	·379	·379	·382	·385	·387	·389	·392	·387	·393	·399	·410	·418	·424
	Oct	·350	·355	·362	·370	·372	·374	·374	·377	·380	·382	·384	·387	·382	·388	·394	·405	·413	·419
	Nov	·352	·357	·364	·372	·374	·376	·376	·379	·382	·384	·386	·389	·384	·390	·396	·407	·415	·421
	Dec	·357	·362	·369	·376	·379	·381	·381	·384	·387	·389	·391	·394	·389	·395	·401	·412	·420	·426
	1993																		
	Jan	·370	·375	·381	·389	·392	·394	·394	·397	·400	·402	·404	·408	·402	·408	·414	·425	·434	·439
	Feb	·361	·366	·372	·380	·383	·385	·385	·388	·391	·393	·395	·398	·393	·399	·405	·416	·424	·430
	Mar	·356	·361	·368	·375	·378	·380	·380	·383	·386	·388	·390	·393	·388	·394	·400	·411	·419	·425
	Apr	·344	·349	·355	·363	·366	·367	·367	·370	·373	·375	·377	·381	·376	·381	·387	·398	·406	·412
	May	·339	·344	·350	·358	·361	·362	·362	·365	·369	·370	·372	·376	·371	·376	·382	·393	·401	·407
	Jun	·340	·345	·351	·359	·362	·363	·363	·366	·370	·371	·373	·377	·372	·377	·383	·394	·402	·408
	Jul	·343	·348	·354	·362	·365	·366	·366	·369	·372	·374	·376	·380	·375	·380	·386	·397	·405	·411
	Aug	·337	·342	·348	·356	·359	·360	·360	·363	·367	·368	·370	·374	·369	·374	·380	·391	·399	·405
	Sep	·331	·336	·342	·350	·353	·354	·354	·357	·361	·362	·364	·368	·363	·369	·374	·385	·393	·399
	Oct	·332	·337	·343	·351	·354	·355	·355	·358	·362	·363	·365	·369	·364	·370	·375	·386	·394	·400
	Nov	·334	·339	·345	·353	·356	·357	·357	·360	·364	·365	·367	·371	·366	·371	·377	·388	·396	·402
	Dec	·331	·336	·342	·350	·353	·354	·354	·357	·361	·362	·364	·368	·363	·369	·374	·385	·393	·399

Indexation allowance — continued

Month of disposal

		2003					2004									
	1994	July	Aug	Sept	Oct	Nov	Dec	Jan	Feb	Mar	Apr	May	June	July	Aug	Sept	Oct	Nov	Dec
B	Jan	·283	·285	·292	·292	·293	·299	·296	·301	·306	·314	·320	·322	·322	·326	·331	·335	·338	·344
a	Feb	·276	·278	·284	·285	·286	·291	·289	·293	·299	·307	·312	·315	·315	·319	·324	·327	·330	·336
s	Mar	·272	·274	·281	·281	·282	·288	·285	·290	·295	·303	·309	·311	·311	·315	·320	·324	·326	·333
e	Apr	·257	·259	·266	·266	·267	·273	·270	·275	·280	·288	·293	·295	·295	·300	·304	·308	·311	·317
	May	·253	·255	·261	·262	·263	·268	·265	·270	·276	·283	·289	·291	·291	·295	·300	·303	·306	·312
M	June	·253	·255	·261	·262	·263	·268	·265	·270	·276	·283	·289	·291	·291	·295	·300	·303	·306	·312
o	July	·259	·261	·267	·268	·269	·274	·272	·276	·282	·290	·295	·297	·297	·301	·306	·310	·313	·319
n	Aug	·253	·255	·261	·262	·263	·268	·265	·270	·276	·283	·289	·291	·291	·295	·300	·303	·306	·312
t	Sept	·250	·252	·259	·259	·260	·266	·263	·268	·273	·281	·286	·288	·288	·292	·297	·301	·303	·310
h	Oct	·249	·251	·257	·258	·258	·264	·261	·266	·271	·279	·284	·287	·287	·291	·295	·299	·302	·308
	Nov	·248	·250	·256	·257	·257	·263	·260	·265	·270	·278	·284	·286	·286	·290	·295	·298	·301	·307
	Dec	·242	·244	·250	·251	·251	·257	·254	·259	·264	·272	·277	·279	·279	·284	·288	·292	·295	·301
	1995																		
	Jan	·242	·244	·250	·251	·251	·257	·254	·259	·264	·272	·277	·279	·279	·284	·288	·292	·295	·301
	Feb	·234	·236	·242	·243	·244	·249	·246	·251	·257	·264	·270	·272	·272	·276	·280	·284	·287	·293
	Mar	·229	·231	·237	·238	·239	·244	·241	·246	·252	·259	·264	·266	·266	·271	·275	·279	·281	·287
	Apr	·217	·219	·225	·226	·226	·232	·229	·234	·239	·246	·252	·254	·254	·258	·262	·266	·268	·274
	May	·212	·214	·220	·221	·221	·227	·224	·229	·234	·241	·247	·249	·249	·253	·257	·261	·263	·269
	June	·210	·212	·218	·219	·220	·225	·222	·227	·232	·240	·245	·247	·247	·251	·256	·259	·262	·268
	July	·216	·218	·224	·225	·225	·231	·228	·233	·238	·245	·251	·253	·253	·257	·262	·265	·268	·274
	Aug	·209	·211	·217	·218	·219	·224	·221	·226	·231	·239	·244	·246	·246	·250	·255	·258	·261	·267
	Sept	·204	·206	·212	·212	·213	·218	·216	·220	·226	·233	·238	·240	·240	·244	·249	·252	·255	·261
	Oct	·210	·212	·218	·219	·220	·225	·222	·227	·232	·240	·245	·247	·247	·251	·256	·259	·262	·268
	Nov	·210	·212	·218	·219	·220	·225	·222	·227	·232	·240	·245	·247	·247	·251	·256	·259	·262	·268
	Dec	·203	·205	·211	·212	·212	·218	·215	·220	·225	·232	·238	·240	·240	·244	·248	·251	·254	·260
	1996																		
	Jan	·207	·209	·215	·216	·216	·222	·219	·224	·229	·236	·242	·244	·244	·248	·252	·256	·258	·264
	Feb	·201	·203	·209	·210	·211	·216	·213	·218	·223	·231	·236	·238	·238	·242	·247	·250	·252	·258
	Mar	·197	·199	·205	·205	·206	·211	·209	·213	·218	·226	·231	·233	·233	·237	·242	·245	·248	·253
	Apr	·188	·190	·196	·197	·197	·202	·200	·204	·210	·217	·222	·224	·224	·228	·233	·236	·239	·244
	May	·186	·188	·194	·194	·195	·200	·198	·202	·207	·215	·220	·222	·222	·226	·230	·233	·236	·242
	June	·185	·187	·193	·193	·194	·199	·197	·201	·207	·214	·219	·221	·221	·225	·229	·233	·235	·241
	July	·190	·192	·198	·198	·199	·204	·201	·206	·211	·219	·224	·226	·226	·230	·234	·238	·240	·246
	Aug	·184	·186	·192	·193	·193	·199	·196	·201	·206	·213	·218	·220	·220	·224	·229	·232	·234	·240
	Sept	·179	·181	·187	·187	·188	·193	·191	·195	·200	·207	·213	·215	·215	·218	·223	·226	·229	·235
	Oct	·179	·181	·187	·187	·188	·193	·191	·195	·200	·207	·213	·215	·215	·218	·223	·226	·229	·235
	Nov	·178	·180	·186	·186	·187	·192	·190	·194	·199	·207	·212	·214	·214	·218	·222	·225	·228	·234
	Dec	·174	·176	·182	·183	·183	·188	·186	·190	·196	·203	·208	·210	·210	·214	·218	·222	·224	·230
	1997																		
	Jan	·174	·176	·182	·183	·183	·188	·186	·190	·196	·203	·208	·210	·210	·214	·218	·222	·224	·230
	Feb	·170	·172	·177	·178	·179	·184	·181	·186	·191	·198	·203	·205	·205	·209	·214	·217	·219	·225
	Mar	·167	·169	·174	·175	·176	·181	·178	·183	·188	·195	·200	·202	·202	·206	·210	·214	·216	·222
	Apr	·160	·162	·168	·168	·169	·174	·171	·176	·181	·188	·193	·195	·195	·199	·203	·207	·209	·215
	May	·156	·157	·163	·164	·164	·170	·167	·171	·177	·184	·189	·191	·191	·194	·199	·202	·205	·210
	June	·151	·153	·159	·159	·160	·165	·163	·167	·172	·179	·184	·186	·186	·190	·194	·197	·200	·206
	July	·151	·153	·159	·159	·160	·165	·163	·167	·172	·179	·184	·186	·186	·190	·194	·197	·200	·206
	Aug	·144	·146	·151	·152	·153	·158	·155	·160	·165	·172	·177	·179	·179	·182	·187	·190	·192	·198
	Sept	·138	·140	·146	·146	·147	·152	·149	·154	·159	·166	·171	·173	·173	·176	·181	·184	·186	·192
	Oct	·137	·139	·144	·145	·145	·150	·148	·152	·157	·164	·169	·171	·171	·175	·179	·182	·185	·191
	Nov	·136	·138	·143	·144	·145	·150	·147	·152	·157	·164	·169	·170	·170	·174	·179	·182	·184	·190
	Dec	·133	·135	·141	·141	·142	·147	·144	·149	·154	·161	·166	·168	·168	·171	·176	·179	·181	·187

Month of disposal

		2005												2006					
	1994	Jan	Feb	Mar	Apr	May	June	July	Aug	Sept	Oct	Nov	Dec	Jan	Feb	Mar	Apr	May	June
B	Jan	·337	·342	·348	·356	·359	·360	·360	·363	·367	·368	·370	·374	·369	·374	·380	·391	·399	·405
a	Feb	·329	·334	·341	·348	·351	·353	·353	·355	·359	·360	·362	·366	·361	·367	·372	·383	·391	·397
s	Mar	·326	·331	·337	·345	·347	·349	·349	·352	·355	·356	·359	·362	·357	·363	·368	·379	·387	·393
e	Apr	·310	·315	·321	·329	·331	·333	·333	·336	·339	·340	·343	·346	·341	·347	·352	·363	·371	·377
	May	·305	·310	·317	·324	·327	·328	·328	·331	·334	·336	·338	·341	·337	·342	·348	·358	·366	·372
M	Jun	·305	·310	·317	·324	·327	·328	·328	·331	·334	·336	·338	·341	·337	·342	·348	·358	·366	·372
o	Jul	·312	·317	·323	·331	·333	·335	·335	·338	·341	·342	·344	·348	·343	·349	·354	·365	·373	·378
n	Aug	·305	·310	·317	·324	·327	·328	·328	·331	·334	·336	·338	·341	·337	·342	·348	·358	·366	·372
t	Sep	·303	·308	·314	·321	·324	·326	·326	·328	·332	·333	·335	·339	·334	·339	·345	·355	·363	·369
h	Oct	·301	·306	·312	·320	·322	·324	·324	·326	·330	·331	·333	·337	·332	·337	·343	·353	·362	·367
	Nov	·300	·305	·311	·319	·321	·323	·323	·326	·329	·330	·332	·336	·331	·337	·342	·352	·361	·366
	Dec	·294	·299	·305	·312	·315	·316	·316	·319	·323	·324	·326	·329	·325	·330	·336	·346	·354	·360
	1995																		
	Jan	·294	·299	·305	·312	·315	·316	·316	·319	·323	·324	·326	·329	·325	·330	·336	·346	·354	·360
	Feb	·286	·291	·297	·304	·307	·308	·308	·311	·314	·316	·318	·321	·317	·322	·327	·338	·346	·351
	Mar	·281	·285	·292	·299	·302	·303	·303	·306	·309	·311	·313	·316	·311	·317	·322	·332	·340	·346
	Apr	·268	·272	·279	·286	·289	·290	·290	·293	·296	·297	·299	·303	·298	·303	·309	·319	·327	·332
	May	·263	·267	·273	·281	·283	·285	·285	·287	·291	·292	·294	·297	·293	·298	·303	·314	·322	·327
	Jun	·261	·266	·272	·279	·282	·283	·283	·286	·289	·290	·292	·296	·291	·296	·302	·312	·320	·325
	Jul	·267	·272	·278	·285	·288	·289	·289	·292	·295	·296	·298	·302	·297	·302	·308	·318	·326	·331
	Aug	·260	·265	·271	·278	·281	·282	·282	·285	·288	·290	·292	·295	·290	·296	·301	·311	·319	·324
	Sep	·254	·259	·265	·272	·275	·276	·276	·279	·282	·284	·286	·289	·284	·290	·295	·305	·313	·318
	Oct	·261	·266	·272	·279	·282	·283	·283	·286	·289	·290	·292	·296	·291	·296	·302	·312	·320	·325
	Nov	·261	·266	·272	·279	·282	·283	·283	·286	·289	·290	·292	·296	·291	·296	·302	·312	·320	·325
	Dec	·253	·258	·264	·271	·274	·275	·275	·278	·281	·283	·285	·288	·283	·289	·294	·304	·312	·317
	1996																		
	Jan	·258	·262	·268	·276	·278	·280	·280	·282	·286	·287	·289	·292	·288	·293	·298	·308	·316	·322
	Feb	·252	·256	·262	·270	·272	·274	·274	·276	·280	·281	·283	·286	·282	·287	·292	·302	·310	·315
	Mar	·247	·251	·257	·265	·267	·269	·269	·271	·275	·276	·278	·281	·277	·282	·287	·297	·305	·310
	Apr	·238	·242	·248	·256	·258	·260	·260	·262	·265	·267	·269	·272	·267	·273	·278	·288	·296	·301
	May	·235	·240	·246	·253	·256	·257	·257	·260	·263	·264	·266	·269	·265	·270	·275	·285	·293	·298
	Jun	·235	·239	·245	·252	·255	·256	·256	·259	·262	·263	·265	·269	·264	·269	·275	·284	·292	·297
	Jul	·240	·244	·250	·257	·260	·261	·261	·264	·267	·268	·270	·274	·269	·274	·280	·289	·297	·302
	Aug	·234	·238	·244	·251	·254	·255	·255	·258	·261	·263	·265	·268	·263	·268	·274	·283	·291	·297
	Sep	·228	·233	·239	·246	·248	·250	·250	·252	·256	·257	·259	·262	·257	·263	·268	·278	·285	·291
	Oct	·228	·233	·239	·246	·248	·250	·250	·252	·256	·257	·259	·262	·257	·263	·268	·278	·285	·291
	Nov	·227	·232	·238	·245	·248	·249	·249	·251	·255	·256	·258	·261	·257	·262	·267	·277	·285	·290
	Dec	·223	·228	·234	·241	·244	·245	·245	·247	·251	·252	·254	·257	·253	·258	·263	·273	·280	·286
	1997																		
	Jan	·223	·228	·234	·241	·244	·245	·245	·247	·251	·252	·254	·257	·253	·258	·263	·273	·280	·286
	Feb	·219	·223	·229	·236	·239	·240	·240	·243	·246	·247	·249	·252	·248	·253	·258	·268	·275	·281
	Mar	·216	·220	·226	·233	·236	·237	·237	·239	·243	·244	·246	·249	·245	·250	·255	·264	·272	·277
	Apr	·209	·213	·219	·226	·228	·230	·230	·232	·235	·237	·239	·242	·237	·242	·248	·257	·265	·270
	May	·204	·208	·214	·221	·224	·225	·225	·228	·231	·232	·234	·237	·233	·238	·243	·252	·260	·265
	Jun	·199	·204	·210	·217	·219	·220	·220	·223	·226	·227	·229	·232	·228	·233	·238	·248	·255	·260
	Jul	·199	·204	·210	·217	·219	·220	·220	·223	·226	·227	·229	·232	·228	·233	·238	·248	·255	·260
	Aug	·192	·196	·202	·209	·211	·213	·213	·215	·218	·220	·221	·225	·220	·225	·230	·240	·247	·252
	Sep	·186	·190	·196	·203	·205	·207	·207	·209	·212	·213	·215	·218	·214	·219	·224	·234	·241	·246
	Oct	·184	·189	·194	·201	·204	·205	·205	·208	·211	·212	·214	·217	·213	·218	·223	·232	·239	·245
	Nov	·184	·188	·194	·201	·203	·204	·204	·207	·210	·211	·213	·216	·212	·217	·222	·231	·239	·244
	Dec	·181	·185	·191	·198	·200	·201	·201	·204	·207	·208	·210	·213	·209	·214	·219	·228	·236	·241

Indexation allowance — continued

Month of disposal

		2003					2004										
	1998	July	Aug	Sept	Oct	Nov	Dec	Jan	Feb	Mar	Apr	May	June	July	Aug	Sept	Oct	Nov	Dec

		July	Aug	Sept	Oct	Nov	Dec	Jan	Feb	Mar	Apr	May	June	July	Aug	Sept	Oct	Nov	Dec
B	Jan	·137	·139	·144	·145	·145	·150	·148	·152	·157	·164	·169	·171	·171	·175	·179	·182	·185	·191
a	Feb	·131	·133	·138	·139	·140	·145	·142	·147	·152	·158	·163	·165	·165	·169	·173	·177	·179	·185
s	Mar	·127	·129	·135	·136	·136	·141	·139	·143	·148	·155	·160	·162	·162	·165	·170	·173	·175	·181
e	Apr	·115	·117	·122	·123	·124	·129	·126	·130	·135	·142	·147	·149	·149	·153	·157	·160	·162	·168
	May	·109	·111	·116	·117	·117	·122	·120	·124	·129	·136	·141	·143	·143	·146	·150	·154	·156	·161
M	June	·110	·111	·117	·118	·118	·123	·121	·125	·130	·136	·141	·143	·143	·147	·151	·154	·157	·162
o	July	·112	·114	·120	·120	·121	·126	·123	·128	·133	·139	·144	·146	·146	·150	·154	·157	·160	·165
n	Aug	·108	·109	·115	·115	·116	·121	·119	·123	·128	·134	·139	·141	·141	·145	·149	·152	·155	·160
t	Sept	·103	·105	·110	·111	·111	·116	·114	·118	·123	·130	·134	·136	·136	·140	·144	·147	·150	·155
h	Oct	·102	·104	·109	·110	·111	·116	·113	·117	·122	·129	·134	·136	·136	·139	·143	·147	·149	·154
	Nov	·103	·105	·110	·111	·111	·116	·114	·118	·123	·130	·134	·136	·136	·140	·144	·147	·150	·155
	Dec	·103	·105	·110	·111	·111	·116	·114	·118	·123	·130	·134	·136	·136	·140	·144	·147	·150	·155
1999																			
	Jan	·110	·111	·117	·118	·118	·123	·121	·125	·130	·136	·141	·143	·143	·147	·151	·154	·157	·162
	Feb	·108	·109	·115	·115	·116	·121	·119	·123	·128	·134	·139	·141	·141	·145	·149	·152	·155	·160
	Mar	·105	·107	·112	·113	·113	·118	·116	·120	·125	·132	·137	·138	·138	·142	·146	·149	·152	·157
	Apr	·097	·099	·105	·105	·106	·111	·108	·113	·117	·124	·129	·131	·131	·134	·139	·142	·144	·150
	May	·095	·097	·102	·103	·103	·108	·106	·110	·115	·121	·126	·128	·128	·132	·136	·139	·141	·147
	June	·095	·097	·102	·103	·103	·108	·106	·110	·115	·121	·126	·128	·128	·132	·136	·139	·141	·147
	July	·098	·100	·105	·106	·107	·111	·109	·113	·118	·125	·130	·131	·131	·135	·139	·142	·145	·150
	Aug	·095	·097	·103	·103	·104	·109	·106	·111	·115	·122	·127	·129	·129	·132	·137	·140	·142	·147
	Sept	·091	·093	·098	·099	·099	·104	·102	·106	·111	·117	·122	·124	·124	·128	·132	·135	·137	·143
	Oct	·089	·091	·096	·097	·097	·102	·100	·104	·109	·115	·120	·122	·122	·126	·130	·133	·135	·141
	Nov	·088	·089	·095	·095	·096	·101	·098	·103	·107	·114	·119	·121	·121	·124	·128	·131	·134	·139
	Dec	·084	·085	·091	·091	·092	·097	·094	·099	·103	·110	·115	·117	·117	·120	·124	·127	·130	·135
2000																			
	Jan	·088	·090	·095	·096	·097	·101	·099	·103	·108	·115	·119	·121	·121	·125	·129	·132	·134	·140
	Feb	·082	·084	·090	·090	·091	·096	·093	·097	·102	·109	·113	·115	·115	·119	·123	·126	·128	·134
	Mar	·077	·078	·084	·084	·085	·090	·087	·091	·096	·103	·107	·109	·109	·113	·117	·120	·122	·128
	Apr	·066	·068	·073	·073	·074	·079	·076	·081	·085	·092	·096	·098	·098	·102	·106	·109	·111	·116
	May	·062	·064	·069	·070	·070	·075	·073	·077	·081	·088	·093	·094	·094	·098	·102	·105	·107	·112
	June	·060	·061	·067	·067	·068	·072	·070	·074	·079	·085	·090	·092	·092	·095	·099	·102	·105	·110
	July	·063	·065	·070	·071	·072	·076	·074	·078	·083	·089	·094	·096	·096	·099	·103	·106	·109	·114
	Aug	·063	·065	·070	·071	·072	·076	·074	·078	·083	·089	·094	·096	·096	·099	·103	·106	·109	·114
	Sept	·056	·058	·063	·063	·064	·069	·066	·070	·075	·082	·086	·088	·088	·091	·096	·098	·101	·106
	Oct	·057	·058	·064	·064	·065	·069	·067	·071	·076	·082	·087	·089	·089	·092	·096	·099	·101	·107
	Nov	·053	·055	·060	·061	·062	·066	·064	·068	·073	·079	·084	·085	·085	·089	·093	·096	·098	·103
	Dec	·053	·055	·060	·060	·061	·066	·063	·067	·072	·078	·083	·085	·085	·088	·092	·095	·098	·103
2001																			
	Jan	·060	·061	·067	·067	·068	·072	·070	·074	·079	·085	·090	·092	·092	·095	·099	·102	·105	·110
	Feb	·054	·056	·061	·062	·062	·067	·065	·069	·073	·080	·084	·086	·086	·090	·094	·097	·099	·104
	Mar	·053	·055	·060	·060	·061	·066	·063	·067	·072	·078	·083	·085	·085	·088	·092	·095	·098	·103
	Apr	·047	·049	·054	·055	·055	·060	·058	·062	·066	·073	·077	·079	·079	·083	·087	·090	·092	·097
	May	·041	·042	·048	·048	·049	·053	·051	·055	·060	·066	·071	·072	·072	·076	·080	·083	·085	·090
	June	·040	·041	·046	·047	·048	·052	·050	·054	·058	·065	·069	·071	·071	·075	·079	·081	·084	·089
	July	·046	·048	·053	·054	·054	·059	·057	·061	·065	·072	·076	·078	·078	·081	·085	·088	·091	·096
	Aug	·042	·044	·049	·049	·050	·055	·052	·056	·061	·067	·072	·074	·074	·077	·081	·084	·086	·091
	Sept	·038	·040	·045	·046	·046	·051	·049	·053	·057	·064	·068	·070	·070	·073	·077	·080	·082	·088
	Oct	·040	·042	·047	·048	·048	·053	·050	·055	·059	·065	·070	·072	·072	·075	·079	·082	·084	·090
	Nov	·044	·046	·051	·052	·052	·057	·055	·059	·063	·070	·074	·076	·076	·079	·084	·086	·089	·094
	Dec	·046	·047	·052	·053	·054	·058	·056	·060	·065	·071	·076	·077	·077	·081	·085	·088	·090	·095

Month of disposal

		2005												2006					
	1998	Jan	Feb	Mar	Apr	May	June	July	Aug	Sept	Oct	Nov	Dec	Jan	Feb	Mar	Apr	May	June
B	Jan	·184	·189	·194	·201	·204	·205	·205	·208	·211	·212	·214	·217	·213	·218	·223	·232	·239	·245
a	Feb	·178	·183	·188	·195	·198	·199	·199	·201	·205	·206	·208	·211	·206	·211	·216	·226	·233	·238
s	Mar	·175	·179	·185	·192	·194	·195	·195	·198	·201	·202	·204	·207	·203	·208	·213	·222	·229	·234
e	Apr	·162	·166	·172	·178	·181	·182	·182	·185	·188	·189	·191	·194	·189	·194	·199	·208	·216	·221
	May	·155	·160	·165	·172	·174	·176	·176	·178	·181	·182	·184	·187	·183	·188	·193	·202	·209	·214
M	Jun	·156	·160	·166	·173	·175	·176	·176	·179	·182	·183	·185	·188	·184	·188	·193	·203	·210	·215
o	Jul	·159	·163	·169	·175	·178	·179	·179	·182	·185	·186	·188	·191	·187	·191	·196	·206	·213	·218
n	Aug	·154	·158	·164	·170	·173	·174	·174	·177	·180	·181	·183	·186	·181	·186	·191	·200	·208	·213
t	Sep	·149	·153	·159	·165	·168	·169	·169	·172	·175	·176	·178	·181	·176	·181	·186	·195	·203	·207
h	Oct	·148	·153	·158	·165	·167	·168	·168	·171	·174	·175	·177	·180	·176	·181	·185	·195	·202	·207
	Nov	·149	·153	·159	·165	·168	·169	·169	·172	·175	·176	·178	·181	·176	·181	·186	·195	·203	·207
	Dec	·149	·153	·159	·165	·168	·169	·169	·172	·175	·176	·178	·181	·176	·181	·186	·195	·203	·207
	1999																		
	Jan	·156	·160	·166	·173	·175	·176	·176	·179	·182	·183	·185	·188	·184	·188	·193	·203	·210	·215
	Feb	·154	·158	·164	·170	·173	·174	·174	·177	·180	·181	·183	·186	·181	·186	·191	·200	·208	·213
	Mar	·151	·155	·161	·168	·170	·171	·171	·174	·177	·178	·180	·183	·179	·183	·188	·197	·205	·210
	Apr	·143	·148	·153	·160	·162	·163	·163	·166	·169	·170	·172	·175	·171	·176	·180	·189	·197	·202
	May	·141	·145	·150	·157	·159	·161	·161	·163	·166	·167	·169	·172	·168	·173	·178	·187	·194	·199
	Jun	·141	·145	·150	·157	·159	·161	·161	·163	·166	·167	·169	·172	·168	·173	·178	·187	·194	·199
	Jul	·144	·148	·154	·161	·163	·164	·164	·167	·170	·171	·173	·176	·171	·176	·181	·190	·197	·202
	Aug	·141	·146	·151	·158	·160	·161	·161	·164	·167	·168	·170	·173	·169	·173	·178	·187	·195	·199
	Sep	·137	·141	·146	·153	·155	·156	·156	·159	·162	·163	·165	·168	·164	·168	·173	·182	·190	·194
	Oct	·135	·139	·144	·151	·153	·154	·154	·157	·160	·161	·163	·166	·162	·166	·171	·180	·187	·192
	Nov	·133	·137	·143	·149	·152	·153	·153	·155	·158	·160	·161	·164	·160	·165	·170	·179	·186	·191
	Dec	·129	·133	·139	·145	·148	·149	·149	·151	·154	·155	·157	·160	·156	·161	·166	·175	·182	·186
	2000																		
	Jan	·134	·138	·143	·150	·152	·154	·154	·156	·159	·160	·162	·165	·161	·166	·170	·179	·187	·191
	Feb	·128	·132	·137	·144	·146	·147	·147	·150	·153	·154	·156	·159	·155	·159	·164	·173	·180	·185
	Mar	·122	·126	·131	·138	·140	·141	·141	·144	·147	·148	·150	·153	·148	·153	·158	·167	·174	·179
	Apr	·111	·115	·120	·126	·129	·130	·130	·132	·135	·136	·138	·141	·137	·142	·146	·155	·162	·167
	May	·107	·111	·116	·122	·125	·126	·126	·128	·131	·132	·134	·137	·133	·138	·142	·151	·158	·163
	Jun	·104	·108	·113	·120	·122	·123	·123	·126	·129	·130	·132	·134	·130	·135	·140	·148	·155	·160
	Jul	·108	·112	·117	·124	·126	·127	·127	·130	·133	·134	·135	·138	·134	·139	·144	·152	·160	·164
	Aug	·108	·112	·117	·124	·126	·127	·127	·130	·133	·134	·135	·138	·134	·139	·144	·152	·160	·164
	Sep	·100	·104	·109	·116	·118	·119	·119	·122	·125	·126	·128	·130	·126	·131	·136	·144	·151	·156
	Oct	·101	·105	·110	·117	·119	·120	·120	·122	·125	·126	·128	·131	·127	·132	·136	·145	·152	·157
	Nov	·098	·102	·107	·113	·116	·117	·117	·119	·122	·123	·125	·128	·124	·128	·133	·142	·149	·153
	Dec	·097	·101	·106	·113	·115	·116	·116	·118	·121	·123	·124	·127	·123	·128	·132	·141	·148	·153
	2001																		
	Jan	·104	·108	·113	·120	·122	·123	·123	·126	·129	·130	·132	·134	·130	·135	·140	·148	·155	·160
	Feb	·098	·102	·108	·114	·116	·117	·117	·120	·123	·124	·126	·128	·124	·129	·134	·142	·149	·154
	Mar	·097	·101	·106	·113	·115	·116	·116	·118	·121	·123	·124	·127	·123	·128	·132	·141	·148	·153
	Apr	·091	·095	·101	·107	·109	·110	·110	·113	·116	·117	·118	·121	·117	·122	·127	·135	·142	·147
	May	·084	·088	·094	·100	·102	·103	·103	·106	·108	·110	·111	·114	·110	·115	·119	·128	·135	·139
	Jun	·083	·087	·092	·099	·101	·102	·102	·104	·107	·108	·110	·113	·109	·114	·118	·127	·134	·138
	Jul	·090	·094	·099	·106	·108	·109	·109	·111	·114	·115	·117	·120	·116	·121	·125	·134	·141	·145
	Aug	·086	·090	·095	·101	·103	·105	·105	·107	·110	·111	·113	·116	·111	·116	·121	·129	·136	·141
	Sep	·082	·086	·091	·097	·100	·101	·101	·103	·106	·107	·109	·112	·108	·112	·117	·125	·132	·137
	Oct	·084	·088	·093	·099	·102	·103	·103	·105	·108	·109	·111	·114	·110	·114	·119	·127	·134	·139
	Nov	·088	·092	·097	·104	·106	·107	·107	·109	·112	·113	·115	·118	·114	·119	·123	·132	·139	·143
	Dec	·089	·093	·099	·105	·107	·108	·108	·111	·114	·115	·116	·119	·115	·120	·125	·133	·140	·145

Indexation allowance — continued

Month of disposal

		2003						2004										
	2002	July	Aug	Sept	Oct	Nov	Dec	Jan	Feb	Mar	Apr	May	June	July	Aug	Sept	Oct	Nov	Dec
B	Jan	·046	·048	·053	·054	·054	·059	·057	·061	·065	·072	·076	·078	·078	·081	·085	·088	·091	·096
a	Feb	·043	·045	·050	·051	·051	·056	·054	·058	·062	·068	·073	·075	·075	·078	·082	·085	·087	·093
s	Mar	·039	·041	·046	·046	·047	·052	·049	·053	·058	·064	·069	·070	·070	·074	·078	·081	·083	·088
e	Apr	·032	·034	·039	·039	·040	·044	·042	·046	·051	·057	·061	·063	·063	·067	·071	·073	·076	·081
	May	·029	·031	·036	·036	·037	·041	·039	·043	·048	·054	·058	·060	·060	·064	·068	·070	·073	·078
M	June	·029	·031	·036	·036	·037	·041	·039	·043	·048	·054	·058	·060	·060	·064	·068	·070	·073	·078
o	July	·031	·032	·038	·038	·039	·043	·041	·045	·049	·056	·060	·062	·062	·065	·069	·072	·074	·080
n	Aug	·028	·029	·035	·035	·036	·040	·038	·042	·046	·053	·057	·059	·059	·062	·066	·069	·071	·077
t	Sept	·021	·023	·028	·028	·029	·033	·031	·035	·039	·046	·050	·052	·052	·055	·059	·062	·064	·069
h	Oct	·019	·021	·026	·026	·027	·031	·029	·033	·038	·044	·048	·050	·050	·053	·057	·060	·062	·067
	Nov	·017	·019	·024	·025	·025	·030	·027	·031	·036	·042	·047	·048	·048	·052	·056	·058	·061	·066
	Dec	·016	·017	·022	·023	·024	·028	·026	·030	·034	·040	·045	·046	·046	·050	·054	·057	·059	·064
	2003																		
	Jan	·016	·018	·023	·024	·024	·029	·026	·030	·035	·041	·045	·047	·047	·050	·054	·057	·059	·064
	Feb	·011	·013	·018	·018	·019	·023	·021	·025	·030	·036	·040	·042	·042	·045	·049	·052	·054	·059
	Mar	·008	·009	·014	·015	·016	·020	·018	·022	·026	·032	·037	·038	·038	·042	·046	·048	·051	·056
	Apr	·001	·002	·007	·008	·008	·013	·010	·014	·019	·025	·029	·031	·031	·034	·038	·041	·043	·048
	May	·000	·001	·006	·006	·007	·011	·009	·013	·017	·023	·028	·029	·029	·033	·036	·039	·041	·046
	June	·000	·002	·007	·007	·008	·012	·010	·014	·018	·024	·029	·030	·030	·034	·038	·040	·042	·047
	July	–	·002	·007	·007	·008	·012	·010	·014	·018	·024	·029	·030	·030	·034	·038	·040	·042	·047
	Aug	–	–	·005	·006	·006	·010	·008	·012	·017	·023	·027	·029	·029	·032	·036	·039	·041	·046
	Sept	–	–	–	·001	·001	·005	·003	·007	·012	·018	·022	·024	·024	·027	·031	·033	·036	·041
	Oct	–	–	–	–	·001	·005	·003	·007	·011	·017	·021	·023	·023	·026	·030	·033	·035	·040
	Nov	–	–	–	–	–	·004	·002	·006	·010	·016	·021	·022	·022	·026	·030	·032	·034	·039
	Dec	–	–	–	–	–	–	·000	·002	·006	·012	·016	·018	·018	·021	·025	·028	·030	·035
	2004																		
	Jan	–	–	–	–	–	–	–	·004	·008	·014	·019	·020	·020	·023	·027	·030	·032	·037
	Feb	–	–	–	–	–	–	–	–	·004	·010	·015	·016	·016	·020	·023	·026	·028	·033
	Mar	–	–	–	–	–	–	–	–	·000	·006	·010	·012	·012	·015	·019	·022	·024	·029
	Apr	–	–	–	–	–	–	–	–	–	·000	·004	·006	·006	·009	·013	·016	·018	·023
	May	–	–	–	–	–	–	–	–	–	–	·000	·002	·002	·005	·009	·011	·013	·018
	June	–	–	–	–	–	–	–	–	–	–	–	·000	·000	·003	·007	·010	·012	·017
	July	–	–	–	–	–	–	–	–	–	–	–	–	·000	·003	·007	·010	·012	·017
	Aug	–	–	–	–	–	–	–	–	–	–	–	–	–	·000	·004	·006	·009	·013
	Sept	–	–	–	–	–	–	–	–	–	–	–	–	–	–	·000	·003	·005	·010
	Oct	–	–	–	–	–	–	–	–	–	–	–	–	–	–	–	·000	·002	·007
	Nov	–	–	–	–	–	–	–	–	–	–	–	–	–	–	–	–	·000	·005
	Dec	–	–	–	–	–	–	–	–	–	–	–	–	–	–	–	–	–	·000
	2005																		
	Jan	–	–	–	–	–	–	–	–	–	–	–	–	–	–	–	–	–	–
	Feb	–	–	–	–	–	–	–	–	–	–	–	–	–	–	–	–	–	–
	Mar	–	–	–	–	–	–	–	–	–	–	–	–	–	–	–	–	–	–
	Apr	–	–	–	–	–	–	–	–	–	–	–	–	–	–	–	–	–	–
	May	–	–	–	–	–	–	–	–	–	–	–	–	–	–	–	–	–	–
	Jun	–	–	–	–	–	–	–	–	–	–	–	–	–	–	–	–	–	–
	July	–	–	–	–	–	–	–	–	–	–	–	–	–	–	–	–	–	–
	Aug	–	–	–	–	–	–	–	–	–	–	–	–	–	–	–	–	–	–
	Sept	–	–	–	–	–	–	–	–	–	–	–	–	–	–	–	–	–	–
	Oct	–	–	–	–	–	–	–	–	–	–	–	–	–	–	–	–	–	–
	Nov	–	–	–	–	–	–	–	–	–	–	–	–	–	–	–	–	–	–
	Dec	–	–	–	–	–	–	–	–	–	–	–	–	–	–	–	–	–	–

Month of disposal

Base Month		2005												2006					
		Jan	Feb	Mar	Apr	May	June	July	Aug	Sept	Oct	Nov	Dec	Jan	Feb	Mar	Apr	May	June
2002	Jan	·090	·094	·099	·106	·108	·109	·109	·111	·114	·115	·117	·120	·116	·121	·125	·134	·141	·145
	Feb	·087	·091	·096	·102	·105	·106	·106	·108	·111	·112	·114	·117	·113	·117	·122	·131	·138	·142
	Mar	·083	·087	·092	·098	·100	·101	·101	·104	·107	·108	·109	·112	·108	·113	·117	·126	·133	·138
	Apr	·075	·079	·084	·090	·093	·094	·094	·096	·099	·100	·102	·105	·101	·105	·110	·118	·125	·130
	May	·072	·076	·081	·087	·090	·091	·091	·093	·096	·097	·099	·102	·098	·102	·107	·115	·122	·127
	Jun	·072	·076	·081	·087	·090	·091	·091	·093	·096	·097	·099	·102	·098	·102	·107	·115	·122	·127
	Jul	·074	·078	·083	·089	·092	·093	·093	·095	·098	·099	·101	·103	·099	·104	·109	·117	·124	·128
	Aug	·071	·075	·080	·086	·088	·090	·090	·092	·095	·096	·098	·100	·096	·101	·105	·114	·121	·125
	Sep	·064	·068	·073	·079	·081	·082	·082	·084	·087	·088	·090	·093	·089	·093	·098	·106	·113	·118
	Oct	·062	·066	·071	·077	·079	·080	·080	·083	·085	·087	·088	·091	·087	·092	·096	·105	·111	·116
	Nov	·060	·064	·069	·075	·077	·079	·079	·081	·084	·085	·086	·089	·085	·090	·094	·103	·109	·114
	Dec	·058	·062	·067	·073	·076	·077	·077	·079	·082	·083	·085	·087	·083	·088	·092	·101	·108	·112
2003	Jan	·059	·063	·068	·074	·076	·077	·077	·080	·082	·084	·085	·088	·084	·089	·093	·101	·108	·113
	Feb	·054	·057	·062	·069	·071	·072	·072	·074	·077	·078	·080	·083	·079	·083	·088	·096	·103	·107
	Mar	·050	·054	·059	·065	·067	·068	·068	·071	·073	·074	·076	·079	·075	·079	·084	·092	·099	·103
	Apr	·042	·046	·051	·057	·060	·061	·061	·063	·066	·067	·068	·071	·067	·072	·076	·084	·091	·095
	May	·041	·045	·050	·056	·058	·059	·059	·061	·064	·065	·067	·069	·066	·070	·074	·083	·089	·094
	Jun	·042	·046	·051	·057	·059	·060	·060	·062	·065	·066	·068	·071	·067	·071	·076	·084	·090	·095
	Jul	·042	·046	·051	·057	·059	·060	·060	·062	·065	·066	·068	·071	·067	·071	·076	·084	·090	·095
	Aug	·040	·044	·049	·055	·057	·058	·058	·061	·063	·064	·066	·069	·065	·069	·074	·082	·089	·093
	Sep	·035	·039	·044	·050	·052	·053	·053	·055	·058	·059	·061	·064	·060	·064	·068	·077	·083	·088
	Oct	·035	·038	·043	·049	·051	·053	·053	·055	·058	·059	·060	·063	·059	·064	·068	·076	·083	·087
	Nov	·034	·038	·043	·049	·051	·052	·052	·054	·057	·058	·060	·062	·059	·063	·067	·076	·082	·086
	Dec	·029	·033	·038	·044	·046	·047	·047	·050	·052	·053	·055	·058	·054	·058	·063	·071	·077	·082
2004	Jan	·032	·035	·040	·046	·049	·050	·050	·052	·055	·056	·057	·060	·056	·061	·065	·073	·080	·084
	Feb	·028	·032	·036	·042	·045	·046	·046	·048	·051	·052	·053	·056	·052	·057	·061	·069	·076	·080
	Mar	·023	·027	·032	·038	·040	·041	·041	·043	·046	·047	·049	·051	·048	·052	·056	·064	·071	·075
	Apr	·017	·021	·026	·032	·034	·035	·035	·037	·040	·041	·043	·045	·041	·046	·050	·058	·065	·069
	May	·013	·017	·021	·027	·029	·031	·031	·033	·035	·036	·038	·041	·037	·041	·046	·054	·060	·064
	Jun	·011	·015	·020	·026	·028	·029	·029	·031	·034	·035	·036	·039	·035	·040	·044	·052	·058	·063
	Jul	·011	·015	·020	·026	·028	·029	·029	·031	·034	·035	·036	·039	·035	·040	·044	·052	·058	·063
	Aug	·008	·012	·017	·022	·025	·026	·026	·028	·030	·031	·033	·036	·032	·036	·041	·049	·055	·059
	Sep	·004	·008	·013	·019	·021	·022	·022	·024	·027	·028	·027	·032	·028	·032	·037	·045	·051	·055
	Oct	·002	·005	·010	·016	·018	·019	·019	·021	·024	·025	·027	·029	·025	·030	·034	·042	·048	·052
	Nov	·000	·003	·008	·014	·016	·017	·017	·019	·022	·023	·024	·027	·023	·028	·032	·040	·046	·050
	Dec	·000	·000	·003	·009	·011	·012	·012	·014	·017	·018	·019	·022	·018	·023	·027	·035	·041	·045
2005	Jan	–	·004	·008	·014	·016	·017	·017	·020	·022	·023	·025	·028	·024	·028	·032	·040	·047	·051
	Feb	–	–	·005	·011	·013	·014	·014	·016	·018	·020	·021	·024	·020	·024	·028	·036	·043	·047
	Mar	–	–	–	·006	·008	·009	·009	·011	·014	·015	·016	·019	·015	·019	·024	·031	·038	·042
	Apr	–	–	–	–	·002	·003	·003	·005	·008	·009	·010	·013	·009	·014	·018	·026	·032	·036
	May	–	–	–	–	–	·001	·001	·003	·006	·007	·008	·011	·007	·011	·016	·023	·030	·034
	Jun	–	–	–	–	–	–	·000	·002	·005	·006	·007	·010	·006	·010	·015	·022	·029	·033
	Jul	–	–	–	–	–	–	–	·002	·005	·006	·007	·010	·006	·010	·015	·022	·029	·033
	Aug	–	–	–	–	–	–	–	–	·003	·004	·005	·008	·004	·008	·012	·020	·026	·031
	Sep	–	–	–	–	–	–	–	–	–	·001	·002	·005	·002	·006	·010	·018	·024	·028
	Oct	–	–	–	–	–	–	–	–	–	–	·002	·004	·001	·005	·009	·017	·023	·027
	Nov	–	–	–	–	–	–	–	–	–	–	–	·003	·000	·003	·007	·015	·021	·025
	Dec	–	–	–	–	–	–	–	–	–	–	–	–	·000	·001	·005	·012	·019	·023
2006	Jan	–	–	–	–	–	–	–	–	–	–	–	–	–	·004	·008	·016	·022	·026
	Feb	–	–	–	–	–	–	–	–	–	–	–	–	–	–	·004	·012	·018	·022
	Mar	–	–	–	–	–	–	–	–	–	–	–	–	–	–	–	·008	·014	·018
	Apr	–	–	–	–	–	–	–	–	–	–	–	–	–	–	–	–	·006	·010
	May	–	–	–	–	–	–	–	–	–	–	–	–	–	–	–	–	–	·004
	Jun	–	–	–	–	–	–	–	–	–	–	–	–	–	–	–	–	–	–

Retail prices index

	Jan	Feb	Mar	Apr	May	June
1982	78·73	78·76	79·44	81·04	81·62	81·85
1983	82·61	82·97	83·12	84·28	84·64	84·84
1984	86·84	87·20	87·48	88·64	88·97	89·20
1985	91·20	91·94	92·80	94·78	95·21	95·41
1986	96·25	96·60	96·73	97·67	97·85	97·79
1987	100·00	100·40	100·60	101·80	101·90	101·90
1988	103·30	103·70	104·10	105·80	106·20	106·60
1989	111·00	111·80	112·30	114·30	115·00	115·40
1990	119·50	120·20	121·40	125·10	126·20	126·70
1991	130·20	130·90	131·40	133·10	133·50	134·10
1992	135·60	136·30	136·70	138·80	139·30	139·30
1993	137·90	138·80	139·30	140·60	141·10	141·00
1994	141·30	142·10	142·50	144·20	144·70	144·70
1995	146·00	146·90	147·50	149·00	149·60	149·80
1996	150·20	150·90	151·50	152·60	152·90	153·00
1997	154·40	155·00	155·40	156·30	156·90	157·50
1998	159·50	160·30	160·80	162·60	163·50	163·40
1999	163·40	163·70	164·10	165·20	165·60	165·60
2000	166·60	167·50	168·40	170·10	170·70	171·10
2001	171·10	172·00	172·20	173·10	174·20	174·40
2002	173·30	173·80	174·50	175·70	176·20	176·20
2003	178·40	179·30	179·90	181·20	181·50	181·30
2004	183·10	183·80	184·60	185·70	186·50	186·80
2005	188·90	189·60	190·50	191·60	192·00	192·20
2006	193·40	194·20	195·00	196·50	197·70	198·50
2007	201·6					

	July	Aug	Sept	Oct	Nov	Dec
1982	81·88	81·90	81·85	82·26	82·66	82·51
1983	85·30	85·68	86·06	86·36	86·67	86·89
1984	89·10	89·94	90·11	90·67	90·95	90·87
1985	95·23	95·49	95·44	95·59	95·92	96·05
1986	97·52	97·82	98·30	98·45	99·29	99·62
1987	101·80	102·10	102·40	102·90	103·40	103·30
1988	106·70	107·90	108·40	109·50	110·00	110·30
1989	115·50	115·80	116·60	117·50	118·50	118·80
1990	126·80	128·10	129·30	130·30	130·00	129·90
1991	133·80	134·10	134·60	135·10	135·60	135·70
1992	138·80	138·90	139·40	139·90	139·70	139·20
1993	140·70	141·30	141·90	141·80	141·60	141·90
1994	144·00	144·70	145·00	145·20	145·30	146·00
1995	149·10	149·90	150·60	149·80	149·80	150·70
1996	152·40	153·10	153·80	153·80	153·90	154·40
1997	157·50	158·50	159·30	159·50	159·60	160·00
1998	163·00	163·70	164·40	164·50	164·40	164·40
1999	165·10	165·50	166·20	166·50	166·70	167·30
2000	170·50	170·50	171·70	171·60	172·10	172·20
2001	173·30	174·00	174·60	174·30	173·60	173·40
2002	175·90	176·40	177·60	177·90	178·20	178·50
2003	181·30	181·60	182·50	182·60	182·70	183·50
2004	186·80	187·40	188·10	188·60	189·00	189·90
2005	192·20	192·60	193·10	193·30	193·60	194·10
2006	198·5	199·2	200·1	200·4	201·1	202·7

Corporation tax

Rates

Financial year	2001	2002	2003	2004	2005	2006
Full rate	30%	30%	30%	30%	30%	30%
Starting rate	10%	0%	0%	0%	0%	—
first relevant amount[1]	£10,000	£10,000	£10,000	£10,000	£10,000	—
second relevant amount[1]	£50,000	£50,000	£50,000	£50,000	£50,000	—
marginal relief fraction	1/40	19/400	19/400	19/400	19/400	—
effective marginal rate*	22.5%	23.75%	23.75%	23.75%	23.75%	—
Small companies' rate	20%	19%	19%	19%	19%	19%
lower relevant amount[1]	£300,000	£300,000	£300,000	£300,000	£300,000	£300,000
upper relevant amount[1]	£1.5m	£1.5m	£1.5m	£1.5m	£1.5m	£1.5m
marginal relief fraction	1/40	11/400	11/400	11/400	11/400	11/400
effective marginal rate*	32.5%	32.75%	32.75%	32.75%	32.75%	32.75%
Non-corporate distribution rate[2]	—	—	—	19%	19%	—
Tax credit: from 6 April[3]	10%	10%	10%	10%	10%	10%

[1] Reduced proportionally for accounting periods of less than 12 months. The limits are divided by the number of associated companies (including the company in question).
[2] Applies where the underlying corporation tax rate is lower than 19% (TA 1988 s 13AB, Sch A2).
[3] Individual shareholders not subject to higher rate tax have no further tax to pay. The abolition of the repayment of tax credit to charities was phased in over five years at 21% for 1999–2000, 17% for 2000–01, 13% for 2001–02, 8% for 2002–03 and 4% for 2003–04.

Marginal relief. The starting and small companies' rate apply to *basic profits* ('I') where *profits* ('P') do not exceed the first or lower relevant amounts. Where *profits* ('P') exceed those amounts but not the second or upper relevant amounts, corporation tax on *basic profits* ('I') is reduced by—

(marginal relief upper profit limit − P) × I/P × fraction, where

P = profits as finally computed for corporation tax purposes *plus* franked investment income excluding franked investment income from UK companies in the same group or consortium of which the recipient is a member

I = profits on which corporation tax is actually borne (income plus chargeable gains).

* Where there is no franked investment income, an alternative to the above formula is to apply the starting or small companies' rate up to the first or lower relevant amount and the effective marginal rates to the balance of the profits.

Reliefs

Corporate Venturing Scheme
(FA 2000 s 63, Schs 15, 16; FA 2001 s 64, Sch 16; FA 2004 s 95, Sch 20; FA 2006 s 91, Sch 14)
In relation to shares issued between 1 April 2000 and 31 March 2010, an investing company can obtain 20% CT relief on amounts subscribed for ordinary shares in small higher-risk unquoted trading companies which are held for at least 3 years. The investor must not own or be entitled to acquire more than 30% of the ordinary shares in the investee company. At least 20% of the shares must be owned by independent individuals. At least 80% (100% before 7 March 2001) of the investment must be employed wholly for the purpose of a relevant trade within 12 months. Chargeable gains on share disposals can be deferred by reinvestment in another shareholding under the scheme. Allowable losses (net of the 20% relief) can be set against income if not deducted from chargeable gains.

Research and development
(FA 2000 ss 68, 69, Schs 19–21; FA 2002 s 53, Sch 12; FA 2003 s 168, Sch 31)
An 'SME' incurring research and development expenditure of at least £10,000 (£25,000 for accounting periods beginning before 27 September 2003) in a 12-month accounting period can obtain relief for 150% of that expenditure. From 1 April 2002, large companies incurring R&D expenditure of at least £10,000 (£25,000 for accounting periods beginning before 9 April 2003) can obtain relief for 125% of that expenditure. Companies not yet in profit or which have not yet started to trade can claim the relief up front as a cash payment. An 'SME' is a company with less than 250 employees and either annual maximum turnover of €50m (€40m for accounting periods ending before 1 January 2005) or annual maximum balance sheet total of €43m (€27m for accounting periods ending before 1 January 2005). See also p 23 for 100% capital allowances for research and development.

Real Estate Investment Trusts (REITs)
(FA 2006 ss 103–145, Schs 16, 17)
From 1 January 2007, qualifying rental income from and gains on disposals of investment properties by UK companies within the REIT scheme will be exempt from corporation tax. See also p 45.

Community investment tax credit see p 59   **Urban regeneration companies** see p 59

Customs levies and taxes

Aggregates Levy

(FA 2001 ss 16–49, Schs 4–10; SI 2004/1959)
Levy on commercial exploitation of aggregates including rock, gravel or sand together with any other substance incorporated or naturally occurring with it. Applies to all aggregate (not recycled) extracted in the UK or territorial waters unless exempt. It does not apply to quarried or mined products such as clay, shale, slate, metal and metal ores, gemstones, semi-precious gemstones and industrial minerals. It is charged at 20% of the full rate for aggregate processed in Northern Ireland until 31.3.2011.

From 1 April 2002	£1.60 per tonne

Climate change levy

(FA 2000 s 30, Sch 6; FA 2006 ss 171, 172)
Levy on supply for industrial or commercial purposes of energy, from 1 April 2001, in the form of electricity, gas, petroleum and hydrocarbon gas supplied in a liquid state, coal and lignite, coke and semi-coke of coal or lignite and petroleum coke.

Taxable commodity supplied	Rate[1]	
	1.4.01–30.3.07	**1.4.07 onwards**
Electricity	0.43p per kWh	0.441p per kWh
Gas supplied by a gas utility or any gas supplied in a gaseous state that is of a kind supplied by a gas utility	0.15p per kWh	0.154p per kWh
Any petroleum gas, or other gaseous hydrocarbon supplied in a liquid state	0.96p per kg	0.985p per kg
Any other taxable commodity	1.17p per kg	1.201p per kg

[1] Rate at which payable if supply is neither a half-rate supply nor a reduced-rate supply. The levy is charged at 20% of the full rate for energy-intensive users. It is charged at half the full rate for horticultural producers until 31 March 2006. Horticultural businesses which sign climate change agreements can benefit from an 80% reduction in the levy in exchange for meeting specific energy efficiency targets.

Insurance premium tax

(FA 1994 ss 48–74, Schs 6A, 7, 7A)
Insurance Premium Tax (IPT) is a tax on premiums received under insurance contracts other than those which are specifically exempt.

	Standard rate	Higher rate[1]
From 1.7.99	5%	17.5%
1.4.97 – 30.6.99	4%	17.5%
1.10.94 – 30.3.97	2.5%	–

[1] The higher rate applies to sales of motor cars, light vans and motorcycles, electrical or mechanical domestic appliances, and travel insurance.

Landfill tax

(FA 1996 ss 39–71, 197, Sch 5; SI 1996/1527; SI 1996/1528)
Tax on disposal of waste imposed on operators of landfill sites calculated by reference to the weight and type of waste deposited in the site. Exemption applies to mining and quarrying waste, dredging waste, pet cemeteries, waste from reclamation of contaminated land and inert waste used to restore licensed landfill sites.

Period	Active waste per tonne	Inert waste per tonne	Maximum credit[1]
1.4.06–31.3.07	£21	£2	6.7%
1.4.05–31.3.06	£18	£2	6%
1.4.04–31.3.05	£15	£2	6.8%
1.4.03–31.3.04	£14	£2	6.5%
1.4.02–31.3.03	£13	£2	20%
1.4.01–31.3.02	£12	£2	20%
1.4.2000–31.3.01	£11	£2	20%

[1] Tax credits are available to operators who make donations to environmental trusts of 90% of the donation to the maximum percentage above of the tax payable in a 12-month period.

Income tax

Starting, basic and higher rates

Band of taxable income £	Band £	Rate %	Tax £	Cumulative tax £
2006–07				
0–2,150	2,150	10	215.00	215.00
2,151–33,300	31,150	22	6,853.00	7,068.00
over 33,300	—	40	—	—
2005–06				
0–2,090	2,090	10	209.00	209.00
2,091–32,400	30,310	22	6,668.20	6,877.20
over 32,400	—	40	—	—
2004–05				
0–2,020	2,020	10	202.00	202.00
2,021–31,400	29,380	22	6,463.60	6,665.60
over 31,400	—	40	—	—
2003–04				
0–1,960	1,960	10	196.00	196.00
1,961–30,500	28,540	22	6,278.80	6,474.80
over 30,500	—	40	—	—
2002–03				
0–1,920	1,920	10	192.00	192.00
1,921–29,900	27,980	22	6,155.60	6,347.60
over 29,900	—	40	—	—
2001–02				
0–1,880	1,880	10	188.00	188.00
1,881–29,400	27,520	22	6,054.40	6,242.40
over 29,400	—	40	—	—

Taxation of savings: Savings income is chargeable at the rates of 10% (if within the starting rate band), 20% and/or 40% (TA 1988 s 1A; FA 2000 s 32).

Savings income includes interest from banks and building societies, interest distributions from authorised unit trusts, interest on gilts and other securities including corporate bonds, purchased life annuities and discounts.

Where income does not exceed the basic rate limit, there will be no further tax to pay on savings income from which the 20% tax rate has been deducted, and any tax over-deducted is repayable. Higher rate taxpayers are liable to pay tax at 40% on that part of their savings income falling above the higher rate limit.

Savings income is generally treated as the second top slice of income behind dividends.

Non-taxpayers may apply to have interest paid without deduction of tax where their total income is expected to be covered by personal allowances. Taxpayers who are entitled to a refund of tax deducted from interest can claim the refund using form R40. HMRC have a *Taxback* website page to simplify repayments: www.hmrc.gov.uk/taxback.

Taxation of dividends: UK and foreign dividends (except those foreign dividends taxed under the remittance basis) form the top slice of taxable income. Where income does not exceed the basic rate limit the rate is 10% (applied to the dividend grossed-up by a tax credit of 1/9th) so that the liability is met by the tax credit. Higher rate taxpayers are liable to pay tax at 32.5% on that part of their dividend income falling above the higher rate limit. See TA 1988 s 1A.

Real Estate Investment Trusts (REITS): From 1 January 2007, distributions paid out of tax exempt property income or gains by UK companies within the REIT scheme are treated as UK property income rather than dividends in the hands of investors and are paid under deduction of basic rate income tax.

Construction industry sub-contractors rate of deduction at source: 18%.

Taxation of trusts

	Rate applicable to trusts	Dividend trust rate
From 2004–05 onwards	40%	32.5%
1999–2000 to 2003–04	34%	25%

From 2005–06 onwards: The first £1,000 for 2006–07 and £500 for 2005–06 of income arising to a trust chargeable at the rate applicable to trusts or the dividend trust rate, is instead chargeable at the basic, lower or dividend ordinary rate depending on the type of income (TA 1988 s 686D; FA 2005 s 14; Budget 2006 BN 35).

Vulnerable beneficiaries: From 2004–05 onwards, trustees can be taxed (on election) on trust income as if it were income of the vulnerable beneficiary taking into account the beneficiary's personal allowances, starting and basic rate bands (FA 2005 ss 23–45).

Table of personal tax reliefs

	2006–07	2005–06
	£	£
Personal allowance (age under 65)	5,035	4,895
Age allowance[1] Total income limit	20,100	19,500
Personal allowance age 65–74	7,280	7,090
Not beneficial if individual's total income exceeds	24,590	23,890
Personal allowance age 75 and over	7,420	7,220
Not beneficial if individual's total income exceeds	24,870	24,150
Married couple's allowance[2,4] Elder partner 65 before 6.4.2000		
Basic allowance	2,350	2,280
Age allowance[3,4] Total income limit	20,100	19,500
Neither partner aged 75 or over	6,065	5,905
Not beneficial if relevant partner[3] under 65 and his total income exceeds	27,530	26,750
65–74 and his total income exceeds	32,020	31,140
Either partner aged 75 and over	6,135	5,975
Not beneficial if relevant partner[3] under 65 and his total income exceeds	27,670	26,890
65–74 and his total income exceeds	32,160	31,280
75 or over and his total income exceeds	32,440	31,540
Children's tax credit[5] Baby rate[6]	—	—
Widow's bereavement allowance[1] (available only where the death occurred before 6 April 2000 and the wife had not remarried before that date)	—	—
Blind person's allowance[7]	1,660	1,610

Notes

[1] The higher age allowances are available if the claimant's total income does not exceed the statutory income limit. Where the total income exceeds the statutory limit, the maximum allowance is reduced by one-half of the excess until it is reduced to the ordinary personal allowance.

[2] The universal married couple's allowance was withdrawn for 2000–01 onwards but continues to be available to any married couple or, from 2005–06, civil partnership where at least one spouse or partner was born before 6 April 1935. The relief is given as a reduction in income tax liability restricted to the lower of 10% of the amount of the allowance or the claimant's total income tax liability.

[3] The higher age allowances are available if the claimant's total income does not exceed the statutory income limit (subject to relief given as a reduction in tax liability as in note 2 above). Where the total income exceeds the statutory limit, the maximum allowance is reduced by one-half of the excess (less any reduction made in the personal age allowance as in note 1 above) but it cannot be reduced to less than the basic couple's allowance.

2004–05	2003–04	2002–03	2001–02	2000–01
£	£	£	£	£
4,745	4,615	4,615	4,535	4,385
18,900	18,300	17,900	17,600	17,000
6,830	6,610	6,100	5,990	5,790
23,070	22,290	20,870	20,510	19,810
6,950	6,720	6,370	6,260	6,050
23,310	22,510	21,410	21,050	20,330
2,210	2,150	2,110	2,070	2,000
18,900	18,300	17,900	17,600	17,000
5,725	5,565	5,465	5,365	5,185
25,930	25,130	24,610	24,190	23,370
30,100	29,120	27,580	27,100	26,180
5,795	5,635	5,535	5,435	5,255
26,070	25,270	24,750	24,330	23,510
30,240	29,260	27,720	27,240	26,320
30,480	29,480	28,260	27,780	26,840
—	—	5,290	5,200	—
—	—	10,490	—	—
—	—	—	—	2,000
1,560	1,510	1,480	1,450	1,400

[4] For marriages entered into before 5 December 2005, married couple's allowance is given to the husband (subject to right of transfer to the wife), the amount of the allowance being determined by the level of the husband's income. For marriages and civil partnerships entered into on or after that date, the allowance is given to whichever of the two partners has the higher total income for the tax year in question, the amount of the allowance being determined by the level of that partner's income (subject to the right to transfer half or all of the basic allowance or excess allowances to the partner). Couples married before 5 December 2005 may make a joint election to be brought within the above rules for couples marrying on or after that date. The election must be made before the start of the first tax year for which it is to have effect. It will continue to have effect for all subsequent tax years and is irrevocable.

[5] The relief is given as a deduction in the tax liability. It is withdrawn at the rate of £2 for every £3 of income chargeable to tax at the higher rate and is restricted to 10% of the resulting figure. From 2003–04 onwards, the relief was replaced by the Child Tax Credit.

[6] For 2002–03 the amount per claimant is higher for the year of birth.

[7] The allowance is available for persons who are registered blind but not for persons registered partially-sighted.

Cars, vans and related benefits

Cars

From 6 April 2002: The income tax charge is based on a percentage of the car's price graduated according to the level of the car's carbon dioxide emissions measured in grams per kilometre (g/km) and rounded down to the nearest 5 g/km: ITEPA 2003 ss 114–148, 169; FA 2003 s 138.

CO_2 emissions in grams per kilometre				% of list price	
2002–03	2003–04	2004–05	2005–06–2007–08	Petrol	Diesel[1]
165	155	145	140	15%	18%
170	160	150	145	16%	19%
175	165	155	150	17%	20%
180	170	160	155	18%	21%
185	175	165	160	19%	22%
190	180	170	165	20%	23%
195	185	175	170	21%	24%
200	190	180	175	22%	25%
205	195	185	180	23%	26%
210	200	190	185	24%	27%
215	205	195	190	25%	28%
220	210	200	195	26%	29%
225	215	205	200	27%	30%
230	220	210	205	28%	31%
235	225	215	210	29%	32%
240	230	220	215	30%	33%
245	235	225	220	31%	34%
250	240	230	225	32%	35%
255	245	235	230	33%	35%
260	250	240	235	34%	35%
265	255	245	240	35%	35%

From 6 April 2008: The level of CO_2 emissions qualifying for the lower rate of 15% will be reduced by 5g/km to 135g/km and the levels for each 1% increment will similarly be reduced by 5g/km. Cars with CO_2 emissions of 120g/km or below will qualify for a lower rate of 10% (FA 2006 s 59).

Cars registered after 28 February 2001

For cars registered on or after 1 March 2001, the definitive CO_2 emissions figure is recorded on the vehicle registration document. For cars first registered between 1 January 1998 and 28 February 2001, the Vehicle Certification Agency supply relevant information on their website at www.vcacarfueldata.org.uk and in their free, twice-yearly edition of the 'New Car Fuel Consumption & Emission Figures' booklet.

Cars registered on or after 1 January 1998 with no CO_2 emission figures

Cylinder capacity of car	Appropriate percentage[1]
1,400cc or less	15%
Over 1,400cc up to 2,000cc	25%
Over 2,000cc	35%
Electrically propelled vehicle	15%

[1] **Diesel cars:** A 3% supplement applies to diesel cars up to a maximum of 35%. The supplement does not apply to diesel cars meeting the Euro IV emissions standards until 5 April 2006 after which time it will apply to such cars registered on or after 1 January 2006.

[2] **Discounts:** Special discounts apply to cars, with or without CO_2 emission figures, registered on or after 1 January 1998: 6% for electrically propelled vehicles, 3% for hybrid electric vehicles (2% before 2006–07) and 2% for gas or bi-fuel cars with CO_2 emission figures for gas (1% before 2006–07).

Cars registered before 1 January 1998 with no CO_2 emission figures: tax is charged on 15% of the list price for engines to 1,400 cc, 22% for engines of 1,401 to 2,000 cc and 32% for engines above 2,000 cc. Cars without a cylinder capacity are taxed on 32% of the list price (15% for electric cars).

List price of car:

(1) Includes any optional accessories supplied with the car when first made available to the employee and any further accessories costing £100 or more (ITEPA 2003 ss 122–131).
(2) Reduced by capital contributions made by the employee (maximum of £5,000) (ITEPA 2003 s 132).
(3) Capped at £80,000 (ITEPA 2003 s 121).
(4) Classic cars (aged 15 years or more and with a market value of £15,000 or more at the end of the year of assessment): substitute market value at end of year of assessment if this is higher than the adjusted list price. £80,000 cap and reduction for capital contributions apply (ITEPA 2003 s 147).

Automatic cars for disabled drivers: CO_2 figure reduced to equivalent for manual car (ITEPA 2003 s 138).

Car unavailable for part of year: Value of the benefit is reduced proportionately (ITEPA 2003 s 143).

National Insurance: Also used to calculate the national insurance contributions payable by employers on the benefit of cars they provide for the private use of their employees, see p 75.

1999–2000 to 2001–02: The income tax charge is based on cash equivalent of a percentage of the car's list price (see below) according to amount of business mileage.

Business miles	Car's age at end of tax year	
	Under 4 years	4 years or more
	% of list price	
Less than 2,500	35	26.25
2,500 but less than 18,000	25	18.75
18,000 or more	15	11.25

The cash equivalent is reduced proportionately where the car is not available for the whole tax year. The amount (as so reduced) is reduced by any payments made by the employee for private use.

List price of car:

(1) Includes qualifying accesssories, excluding accessories provided after car made available if its list price was less than £100. Accessories designed for use only by disabled people also excluded. Where a car is manufactured so as to be capable of running on road fuel gas, its price is proportionately reduced by so much of that price as is reasonably attributable to it being manufactured in that way. Where a new car is converted to run on road fuel gas, the equipment is not regarded as an accessory.
(2) Reduced by capital contributions made by employee up to £5,000.
(3) List price as adjusted capped at £80,000.
(4) Classic cars (aged 15 years or more and with a market value of £15,000 or more at end of tax year): substitute market value at end of tax year if higher than adjusted list price. £80,000 cap and reduction for capital contributions apply.
(5) Mileage figures are reduced proportionately where car is not available for whole year.
(6) For second and subsequent cars there is no reduction if business mileage is under 18,000 miles; **from 1999–2000** reduce basic cash equivalent to 25% if business mileage is 18,000 miles or more.

Vans
(ITEPA 2003 ss 114–118, 154–166, 168, 169A, 170)

	Van's age at end of tax year	
	Under 4 years	4 years or more
1993–94 to 2006–07: Vehicle weight up to 3,500 kgs	£500	£350

The charge also covers provision of fuel.
From 6 April 2005 no charge applies to employees who have to take their van home and private use is restricted other than for ordinary commuting (insignificant use is disregarded).
From 6 April 2007 the scale charge will increase to £3,000 irrespective of the age of the van. An additional fuel charge of £500 will also apply for unrestricted private use (FA 2004 s 80, Sch 14).

Related benefits

Parking facilities: No taxable benefit for work place provision of car parking spaces, or parking for bicycles or motorcycles or, from 6 April 2005, vans (ITEPA 2003 s 237).
Cycles and cyclist's safety equipment: No taxable benefit in respect of the provision to employees of bicycles or cycling safety equipment for travel to and from work (ITEPA 2003 s 244) nor, from 6 April 2005, for subsequent transfer to the employee at market value (ITEPA 2003 s 206).
On-call emergency vehicles: From 6 April 2004 onwards no tax or NIC charge where emergency service workers have private use of their emergency vehicle when on call (ITEPA 2003 s 248A).
Bus services: From 6 April 2002 onwards no taxable benefit in respect of the provision of works buses with a seating capacity of 9 or more, provided to employees (or their children) to travel to and from work (ITEPA 2003 s 242). (Before 5 April 2002 the minimum seating capacity was 12.) From 6 April 2002 no tax or NIC charge where employees are carried free or at reduced rates on employer-subsidised local bus services (ITEPA 2003 s 243).

Car and motorcycle hire: restricted allowances
(TA 1988 ss 578A, 578B; ITTOIA 2005 ss 48–50)
If a car with a retail price when new of more than £12,000 is acquired under a rental lease the maximum allowable deduction in computing trading profits is restricted to —

$$\frac{£12,000 + P}{2P} \times R$$

P = retail price of car when new   R = annual rental

Capital allowances see p 23.

Cars, vans and related benefits — continued

Car fuel: company cars

(ITEPA 2003 ss 149–153; TA 1988 s 158)

For 2003–04 onwards, the same percentage figures on page 48 used to calculate the car benefit charge for the company car, which are directly linked to the car's CO_2 emissions, are used to calculate the benefit charge for fuel provided for private motoring. The relevant percentage figure is multiplied by £14,400 for 2003–04 to 2006–07.

CO_2 emissions grams per kilometre			Petrol	Diesel
2003–04	2004–05	2005–06–2006–07	£	£
155	145	140	2,160	2,592
160	150	145	2,304	2,736
165	155	150	2,448	2,880
170	160	155	2,592	3,024
175	165	160	2,736	3,168
180	170	165	2,880	3,312
185	175	170	3,024	3,456
190	180	175	3,168	3,600
195	185	180	3,312	3,744
200	190	185	3,456	3,888
205	195	190	3,600	4,032
210	200	195	3,744	4,176
215	205	200	3,888	4,320
220	210	205	4,032	4,464
225	215	210	4,176	4,608
230	220	215	4,320	4,752
235	225	220	4,464	4,896
240	230	225	4,608	5,040
245	235	230	4,752	5,040
250	240	235	4,896	5,040
255	245	240	5,040	5,040

The benefit is reduced to nil if the employee is required to, and does, make good all fuel provided for private use. There is no taxable benefit where the employer only provides fuel for business travel. From 2003–04, the charge is proportionately reduced where the employee stops receiving free fuel part way through the tax year, but where free fuel is subsequently provided in the same tax year, the full year's charge is payable.

The benefit is proportionately reduced where a car is not available or is incapable of being used for part of a year (being at least 30 days).

2002–03		
Cylinder capacity: (non-diesel cars)	1,400cc or less Over 1,400cc up to 2,000cc Over 2,000cc	£2,240 £2,850 £4,200
Cylinder capacity: (diesel cars)	2,000cc or less Over 2,000cc	£2,850 £4,200
No internal combustion engine		£4,200
2001–02		
Cylinder capacity: (non-diesel cars)	1,400cc or less Over 1,400cc up to 2,000cc Over 2,000cc	£1,930 £2,460 £3,620
Cylinder capacity: (diesel cars)	2,000cc or less Over 2,000cc	£2,460 £3,620
No internal combustion engine		£3,620
2000–01		
Cylinder capacity: (non-diesel cars)	1,400cc or less Over 1,400cc up to 2,000cc Over 2,000cc	£1,700 £2,170 £3,200
Cylinder capacity: (diesel cars)	2,000cc or less Over 2,000cc	£2,170 £3,200
No internal combustion engine		£3,200

Mileage allowances

Advisory fuel rates for company cars

Engine size	Cost per mile		
	Petrol	Diesel	LPG
From 1 July 2006			
1,400cc or less	11p	10p	7p
1,401–2,000cc	13p	10p	8p
Over 2,000cc	18p	14p	11p
1.7.05–30.6.06			
1,400cc or less	10p	9p	7p
1,401–2,000cc	12p	9p	8p
Over 2,000cc	16p	13p	10p
6.4.04–30.6.05			
1,400cc or less	10p	9p	7p
1,401–2,000cc	12p	9p	8p
Over 2,000cc	14p	12p	10p
2002–03 and 2003–04[1]			
1,400cc or less	10p	9p	6p
1,401–2,000cc	12p	9p	7p
Over 2,000cc	14p	12p	9p

Notes
[1] Advisory fuel rates can be used to negotiate dispensations for mileage payments from 28 January 2002 where:
   (a) employers reimburse employees for business travel in their company cars; or
   (b) employers require employees to repay the cost of fuel used for private travel.
   (In the case of (b) the figures may be used for reimbursements of private travel from 6 April 2001.)
[2] Payments at or below these rates are tax and NIC free. The table figures will be accepted for VAT purposes.
[3] Other rates may be used if the employer can demonstrate that they are justified.
[4] The rates will be reviewed if fuel prices vary by more than 10% from the prices used when the rates were set.

Authorised mileage rates

	Rate per business mile	
Cars		
	First 10,000 miles	Over 10,000 miles
2002–03 onwards[1]	40p	25p
2001–02[2]		
Engine size	First 4,000 miles	Over 4,000 miles
Up to 1,500 cc	40p	25p
1,501–2,000 cc	45p	25p
Over 2,000 cc	63p	36p
Fixed rate	42.5p	25p
Car passengers		
Allowance for each fellow passenger carried		
2002–03 onwards[1]		5p
Cycles and motorcycles		
	Cycles	Motorcycles
2002–03 onwards[1]	20p	24p
2000–01–2001–02	12p	24p

[1] Where the employer pays less than the authorised rate the employee can claim tax relief for the difference (ITEPA ss 229–232, 235, 236).
[2] Up to 2001–02, simplified arrangements could be operated known as the Fixed Profit Car Scheme (FPCS) or the Car Allowances Enhanced Reporting Scheme (CAERS), under which an employee's taxable business mileage profit was determined by reference to the engine size and the excess of the mileage allowance paid over the authorised rates.

Charities

Gift Aid scheme
Under the Gift Aid scheme an individual donor can claim higher rate relief on the grossed up amount of a monetary donation against income tax and capital gains tax. The charity claims basic rate relief on the grossed up amount of the donation. Donors must make a declaration that they are UK taxpayers to allow the charity to reclaim the repayment. One declaration can cover a series of donations to the same charity and the declaration can be made by writing, by electronic means or orally. A declaration can be backdated for up to six years prior to the declaration for donations made after 5 April 2000. The basic rate tax deemed to have been deducted by the donor at source is clawed back if the donor's tax liability is insufficient to match it.

Donors may elect in their self-assessment tax returns for donations made after 5 April 2003 to be treated as made in the preceding tax year for higher rate relief purposes. From April 2004, taxpayers can nominate a charity to receive all or part of any tax repayment due to them. The nomination is made on the taxpayer's self-assessment tax return for 2003–04 and later years, with an indication of whether Gift Aid should apply to the donation.

From 6 April 2002, the scheme is extended to gifts to Community Amateur Sports Clubs.

Relief for payments falling due after 5 April 2000 under charitable covenants is given under the Gift Aid scheme. (FA 1990 s 25; FA 2000 ss 39, 40; FA 2002 ss 58, 98; FA 2004 s 83)

Gifts in kind
Relief is available for gifts by traders to educational establishments of goods produced or sold or of plant or machinery used for the purposes of the trade (TA 1988 ss 83A, 84; CAA 2001 s 63(2)–(4); ITTOIA 2005 ss 107–109).

Gifts of shares and securities
Relief is available where a person disposes of listed shares and securities, unit trust units, AIM shares, etc to a charity by way of a gift or sale at an undervalue. The amount deductible from total income is the market value of the shares etc on the date of disposal plus incidental disposal costs less any consideration or value of benefits received by the donor or a connected person. This is in addition to any capital gains tax relief (TA 1988 s 587B; FA 2000 s 43).

Gifts of real property
From 6 April 2002 (1 April 2002 for companies), the relief described immediately above is available for gifts of freehold or leasehold property which a charity agrees to accept (FA 2002 s 97).

Payroll giving
Under the payroll giving scheme, employees authorise their employer to deduct charitable donations from their pay and receive tax relief on their donation at their top rate of tax. The government added a supplement to donations from 6 April 2000 to 5 April 2004. From 6 April 2004 to 31 December 2006, the first £10 donated by each employee every month will be matched for a period of six months. (FA 2000 s 38; FA 2003 s 148; ITEPA 2003 ss 713–715; SI 1986 No 2211).

Inheritance tax relief see p 70.

Capital gains tax see p 28.

Employment benefits

The following benefits on pages 53 to 55 cover some common benefits not detailed separately elsewhere. References to 'lower-paid' employees are to those whose annual remuneration plus benefits is less than £8,500.

Accommodation, supplies, etc used in employment duties
(ITEPA 2003 s 316)

The provision of accommodation, supplies or services used by employees in performance of employment duties is not taxable provided:
(a) if the benefit is provided on premises occupied by the employer, any private use by the employee (or the employee's family or household) is not significant; or
(b) in any other case, the sole purpose of providing the benefit is to enable the employee to perform those duties, any private use is not significant and the benefit is not an excluded benefit (eg the provision of a motor vehicle, boat or aircraft).

Assets given to employees
(ITEPA 2003 ss 203, 204)

If new, tax is chargeable on the cost to the employer (market value in the case of a 'lower-paid' employee). If used, tax is chargeable on the greater of:
(a) market value at the time of transfer; and
(b) where the asset is first applied for the provision of a benefit after 5.4.80 and a person has been chargeable to tax on its use, market value when first so applied less amounts charged to tax for use up to and including the year of transfer.

Buses to shops
(SI 2002/205)

From 6 April 2002, the provision of buses for journeys of 10 miles or less from the workplace to shops etc on a working day is not taxable.

Cheap loans
(ITEPA 2003 ss 174–190)

A taxable benefit arises on employer-related loans to directors or employees earning £8,500 or more a year, on the difference between the interest paid and interest payable at the 'official rate' below. There is no tax charge where:
(a) all the employer-related loans (or all loans not qualifying for tax relief) do not exceed £5,000;
(b) all the interest payable is or would be eligible for tax relief; and
(c) the loans are ordinary commercial loans.

The 'official rate' is:

From 6 January 2002	5%
From 6 March 1999 to 5 January 2002	6.25%

The average rate for the tax year is:

2002–03 to 2006–07	5%
2001–2002	5.94%
1999–2000 to 2000–01	6.25%

From 2000–01 the official rate is set in advance for the whole of the following tax year, subject to review if the typical mortgage rates were to fall sharply during a tax year.

Christmas parties and annual functions
(ITEPA 2003 s 264; SI 2003/1361)

Not taxable if cost does not exceed £150 per head per tax year (£75 for 2002–03 and earlier) and open to staff generally. Otherwise, fully taxable. Expenditure may be split between more than one function. (Not taxable on 'lower-paid' employees.)

Employment benefits — continued

Childcare provision
(ITEPA 2003 ss 318–318D; SI 2006/882)
From 2005–06, no liability arises:
(a) where the premises (which are not wholly or mainly used as a private dwelling) are made available by the employer or, where the scheme is provided under arrangements with other persons, by one or more of those persons; or
(b) where (a) does not apply, to the first £55 per week from 2006–07 or the first £50 per week for 2005–06 of registered or approved childcare.
Before 2005–06, broadly similar provisions to (a) applied.

Disabled employees
(ITEPA 2003 ss 246, 247; SI 2002/1596)
The provision of or payment for transport for disabled employees for ordinary commuting is tax free. From 9 July 2002, this also applies to the provision of equipment, services or facilities to disabled employees to help them carry out their duties of employment.

Eye tests and corrective appliances
(ITEPA 2003 s 320A; FA 2006 s 62)
From 2006–07, no liability arises where the provision of tests or special corrective appliances are required under health and safety legislation and are available as required to employees generally.

Homeworkers
(ITEPA 2003 s 316A)
From 2003–04, employer contributions to additional household costs not taxable where employee works at home. Supporting evidence required if contributions exceed £2 per week (£104 per year).

Incidental overnight expenses
(ITEPA 2003 ss 99–108)
Not taxable where employee stays away from home on business and payment from employer does not exceed
(a) £5 per night in the UK; or
(b) £10 per night overseas.

Living accommodation
A taxable benefit (the '*basic charge*') arises on the annual rental value (or actual rent if greater) less any sums made good by the employee. There is an *additional charge* (if the basic charge is not calculated on the full open market rental value) where the cost of accommodation (including costs of any capital improvements less amounts made good by the employee) exceeds £75,000. The additional charge is the excess cost over £75,000 multiplied by the official rate for cheap loans (see above) in force at the start of the tax year less any rent paid by the employee in excess of the basic charge.

The charges are apportioned in the case of multiple occupation or if the property is provided for only part of the year or part is used exclusively for business purposes.

Exemption: No taxable benefit arises where living accommodation is provided:
(a) for the proper performance of duties;
(b) by reason that it is customary to do so; or
(c) by reason of special threat to the employee's security.

The above exemptions apply to a full-time working director whose interest in the company does not exceed 5%, otherwise only exemption (c) applies to directors.

Living expenses
(ITEPA 2003 ss 313–315)
A taxable charge arises on the cost to the employer of the employee's living expenses. For the provision of assets such as furniture, see 'Use of employer's assets' on page 55.

Where the exemption for living accommodation above applies, the tax charge relating to living expenses (including the provision of furniture and items normal for domestic occupation) is restricted to 10% of the employee's net earnings from the related employment less any sums made good by the employee.

Expenditure on alteration and structural repairs which are normally the landlord's responsibility do not give rise to a taxable benefit.

Long service awards
(ITEPA 2003 s 323; SI 2003/1361)
Not taxable provided the employee has at least 20 years' service and cost to the employer does not exceed £50 (£20 where made before 13.6.03) for each year of service. No similar award may be be made within 10 years of such an award.

Meals
(ITEPA 2003 s 317)
Subsidised or free meals provided for staff generally at the workplace are not taxable.

Medical check-ups and insurance
(ITEPA 2003 s 325; HMRC Employment Income Manual EIM 21765)
Routine health checks and medical screenings for employee (or members of the family or household) are not taxable. Insurance premiums paid on behalf of employees (other than 'lower-paid' employees) are taxable unless for treatment outside the UK whilst the employee is performing duties abroad.

Personal expenses
(ITEPA 2003 ss 70–72, 336–340)
Unless covered by specific exemptions, payments to an employee by reason of his employment in respect of expenses or allowances, are taxable. Deduction is allowed for expenses the employee is obliged to incur which are:
(a) qualifying travelling expenses (broadly those necessarily incurred other than for ordinary commuting or private travel); or
(b) other amounts incurred wholly, exclusively and necessarily in the performance of employment duties.

Relocation expenses
(ITEPA 2003 ss 271–289)
Qualifying removal expenses and benefits up to £8,000 per move in connection with job-related residential moves are not taxable. Included are expenses of disposal, acquisition, abortive acquisition, transport of belongings, travelling and subsistence, bridging loans and duplicate expenses (replacement domestic items).

Third party gifts
(ITEPA 2003 ss 270, 324; SI 2003/1361)
Gifts during the tax year of goods and non-cash vouchers up to £250 (£150 for 2002–03 and earlier years) not taxable where provided by a party unconnected with the employer and not for services provided in connection with employment.

Use of employer's assets
(ITEPA 2003 ss 203–206, 242, 244, 320; FA 2005 s 17; FA 2006 ss 60, 61)
Tax is chargeable on the annual rental value of land and, for other assets, at 20% of the market value when they are first lent or the rental charge to the employer if higher. No taxable benefit arises on:
(a) the loan of a mobile phone for private use (from 6 April 2006 this is restricted to one mobile phone per employee and no longer extends to the employee's family or household but phones first loaned before 6 April 2006 are not affected by the change);
(b) the use of works buses (see p 49);
(c) bicycles and cycle safety equipment (see p 49);
(d) to 5 April 2006, the loan of computer equipment for private use, provided use is not restricted to directors or senior staff and value of benefit does not exceed £2,500 (computers made available for private use before 6 April 2006 are not affected by the change).
From 6 April 2005, no benefit arises on the subsequent purchase by an employee at market value of computer or cycling equipment previously on loan.

Vouchers
(ITEPA 2003 ss 73–89, 95, 96, 268–270, 362)
Vouchers are taxable as follows.
(a) Cash vouchers   On amount for which voucher can be exchanged
(b) Non-cash vouchers   On cost to employer less any contribution from employee (except where used to obtain certain non-taxable benefits)
(c) Luncheon vouchers   On excess over 15p per working day
(d) Transport vouchers   On cost to employer less any contribution from employee

Employment income

PAYE and national insurance thresholds

	2001–02	2002–03	2003–04	2004–05	2005–06	2006–07
	£	£	£	£	£	£
Weekly	87	89	89	91	94	97
Monthly	378	385	385	395	408	420

National minimum wage
(Hourly rate)

Age of worker	Under 18*	18–21**	22 or more
1.10.05–30.9.06	£3.00	£4.25	£5.05
1.10.04–30.9.05	£3.00	£4.10	£4.85
1.10.03–30.9.04	–	£3.80	£4.50

* Applies to all workers under 18 who are no longer of compulsory school age.
** Also applies to workers aged 22 or more, starting a new job with a new employer, doing accredited training.

Basis of assessment
(ITEPA 2003 ss 14–43)

	Services performed			
Persons domiciled in UK	Wholly in UK	Partly in UK	Partly abroad	Wholly abroad
Non-resident	All	That part	None	None
Resident but not ordinarily resident	All	That part	Remittances	Remittances
Resident and ordinarily resident	All	All*	All*	All*
Persons domiciled outside the UK				
UK employer	As for person domiciled in the UK			
Foreign employer				
Non-resident	All UK earnings			
Resident but not ordinarily resident	All UK earnings and remittances for duties performed outside UK			
Resident and ordinarily resident	Remittances for duties performed outside UK			

* Exemption for seafarers if at least half of qualifying period of over 364 days worked abroad (including 183 consecutive days) (FA 1998 s 63; ITEPA 2003 ss 378–385).

Termination payments

The following lump sum payments are exempt from tax.
(a) Payments in connection with the cessation of employment on the death, injury or disability of the employee.
(b) Payments under unapproved retirement benefits schemes where the employee has been taxed on the actual or notional contributions to provide the benefit.
(c) Payments under approved retirement benefits schemes which can properly be regarded as a benefit earned by past service.
(d) Certain payments of terminal grants to members of the armed forces.
(e) Certain benefits under superannuation schemes for civil servants in Commonwealth overseas territories.
(f) Payments in respect of foreign service where the period of foreign service comprises –
  (i) 75% of the whole period of service; or
  (ii) the whole of the last 10 years of service; or
  (iii) where the period of service exceeded 20 years, one-half of that period, including any 10 of the last 20 years.
Otherwise, a proportion of the payment is exempt, as follows –

$$\frac{\text{length of foreign service}}{\text{length of total service}} \times \text{amount otherwise chargeable}$$

(g) The first £30,000 of genuine ex gratia payments (where there is no 'arrangement' by the employer to make the payment): ITEPA 2003 ss 401–413.
(h) Statutory redundancy payments (included in computing £30,000 limit in (g) above).

Fixed rate expenses

For most classes of industry fixed rate allowances for the upkeep of tools and special clothing have been agreed between HMRC and the trade unions concerned. Alternatively, the individual employee may claim as a deduction his or her actual expenses (ITEPA 2003, s 367). (HMRC Employment Income Manual, EIM 32712).

Industry	Occupation	Deduction from 2004–05
Agriculture	All workers	70
Aluminium (Note (2))	(a) Continual casting operators, process operators, de-dimplers, driers, drill punchers, dross unloaders, firemen, furnace operators and their helpers, leaders, mouldmen, pourers, remelt department labourers, roll flatteners (b) Cable hands, case makers, labourers, mates, truck drivers and measurers, storekeepers (c) Apprentices (d) All other workers	130 60 45 100
Banks and Building Societies	Uniformed doormen and messengers (£40 before 2004/05)	45
Brass and Copper	Braziers, coppersmiths, finishers, fitters, moulders, turners and all other workers	100
Building	(a) Joiners and carpenters (b) Cement works, roofing felt and asphalt labourers (c) Labourers and navvies (£40 before 2004/05) (d) All other workers	105 55 45 85
Building Materials	(a) Stone masons (b) Tilemakers and labourers (£40 before 2004/05) (c) All other workers	85 45 55
Clothing	(a) Lacemakers, hosiery bleachers, dyers, scourers and knitters, knitwear bleachers and dyers (b) All other workers (£30 before 2004/05)	45 45
Constructional Engineering (Note (3))	(a) Blacksmiths and their strikers, burners, caulkers, chippers, drillers, erectors, fitters, holders up, markers off, platers, riggers, riveters, rivet heaters, scaffolders, sheeters, template workers, turners, welders (b) Banksmen, labourers, shop-helpers, slewers, straighteners (c) Apprentices and storekeepers (d) All other workers	115 60 45 75
Electrical and Electricity Supply	(a) Those workers incurring laundry costs only (£25 before 2004/05) (b) All other workers	45 90
Engineering (trades ancillary to)	(a) Pattern makers (b) Labourers, supervisory and unskilled workers (c) Apprentices and storekeepers (d) Motor mechanics in garage repair shops (e) All other workers	120 60 45 100 100
Fire service	Uniformed fire fighters and fire officers	60
Food	All workers (£40 before 2004/05)	45
Forestry	All workers	70
Glass	All workers	60
Healthcare staff in the NHS, private hospitals and nursing homes	(a) Ambulance staff on active service (b) Nurses and midwives, chiropodists, dental nurses, occupational, speech and other therapists, phlebotomists and radiographers (c) Plaster room orderlies, hospital porters, ward clerks, sterile supply workers, hospital domestics, hospital catering staff (d) Laboratory staff, pharmacists, pharmacy assistants (e) Uniformed ancillary staff: maintenance workers, grounds staff, drivers, parking attendants and security guards, receptionists and other uniformed staff	110 70 60 45 45
Heating	(a) Pipe fitters and plumbers (b) Coverers, laggers, domestic glaziers, heating engineers and their mates (c) All gas workers, all other workers	100 90 70
Iron Mining	(a) Fillers, miners and underground workers (b) All other workers	100 75

Fixed rate expenses — continued

Industry	Occupation	Deduction from 2004–05
Iron and Steel	(a) Day labourers, general labourers, stockmen, time keepers, warehouse staff and weighmen (b) Apprentices (c) All other workers	60 45 120
Leather	(a) Curriers (wet workers), fellmongering workers, tanning operatives (wet) (b) All other workers (£40 before 2004/05)	55 45
Particular Engineering (Note (4))	(a) Pattern makers (b) Chainmakers; cleaners, galvanisers, tinners and wire drawers in the wire drawing industry; tool-makers in the lock making industry (c) Apprentices and storekeepers (d) All other workers	120 100 45 60
Police Force	Uniformed police officers (ranks up to and including Chief Inspector)	55
Precious Metals	All workers	70
Printing	(a) Letterpress Section — electrical engineers (rotary presses), electrotypers, ink and roller makers, machine minders (rotary), maintenance engineers (rotary presses) and stereotypers (b) Bench hands (periodical and bookbinding section), compositors (letterpress section), readers (letterpress section), telecommunications and electronic section wire room operators, warehousemen (paper box making section) (£30 before 2004/05) (c) All other workers	105 45 70
Prisons	Uniformed prison officers	55

Public Service	(i) Dock and Inland Waterways
	   (a) Dockers, dredger drivers, hopper steerers
	   (b) All other workers (£40 before 2004/05)
	(ii) Public Transport
	   (a) Garage hands (including cleaners)
	   (b) Conductors and drivers (£40 before 2004/05)
		
		55
		45
		
		55
		45

Quarrying	All workers	70
Railways	(See the appropriate category for craftsmen, e.g. engineers, vehicles etc.) All other workers	70
Seamen	Carpenters (a) Passenger liners (£135 before 2004/05) (b) Cargo vessels, tankers, coasters and ferries	 165 130
Shipyards	(a) Blacksmiths and their strikers, boilermakers, burners, carpenters, caulkers, drillers, furnacemen (platers), holders up, fitters, platers, plumbers, riveters, sheet iron workers, shipwrights, tubers, welders (b) Labourers (c) Apprentices and storekeepers (d) All other workers	115 60 45 75
Textiles and Textile Printing	(a) Carders, carding engineers, overlookers and technicians in spinning mills (b) All other workers	85 60
Vehicles	(a) Builders, railway vehicle repairers, and railway wagon lifters (b) Railway vehicle painters and letterers, builders' and repairers' assistants (c) All other workers (£40 before 2004/05)	105 60 45
Wood & Furniture	(a) Carpenters, cabinet makers, joiners, wood carvers and woodcutting machinists (b) Artificial limb makers (other than in wood), organ builders and packing case makers (c) Coopers not providing own tools, labourers, polishers and upholsterers (d) All other workers	115 90 45 75

Notes:
(1) The expressions 'all workers' and 'all other workers' refer only to manual workers who have to bear the cost of upkeep of tools and special clothing. They do not extend to other employees such as office staff.
(2) The term 'firemen' means persons engaged to light and maintain furnaces.
(3) 'Constructional engineering' means engineering undertaken on a construction site, including buildings, shipyards, bridges, roads and other similar operations.
(4) 'Particular engineering' means engineering undertaken on a commercial basis in a factory or workshop for the purposes of producing components such as wire, springs, nails and locks.

Investment reliefs

Community investment tax credit
(FA 2002 s 57, Sch 16)
Investments made after 16 April 2002 by an individual or company in an accredited community development finance institution (CDFI) are eligible for tax relief up to 25%. The investment may be a loan or a subscription for shares or securities. Tax relief may be claimed for the tax year in which the investment is made and each of the four subsequent years. Relief for each year is the smaller of 5% of the invested amount, or the amount which reduces the investor's income tax liability for the year to nil.

Enterprise investment scheme
(TA 1988 ss 289–312; FA 1997 Sch 8; FA 2000 Sch 17; FA 2004 Sch 18; FA 2006 s 91, Sch 14)
The EIS applies to investments in qualifying unquoted companies trading in the UK. Eligible shares must be held for at least 3 years from the issue date or commencement of trade if later (5 years from the issue date for shares issued before 6 April 2000). The following reliefs apply subject to this and other conditions.

Relief on investment

Maximum investment:	From 2006–07 2004–05 to 2005–06 1998–99 to 2003–04	£400,000 £200,000 £150,000
Minimum investment:	From 1993–94	£500
Maximum carry-back to preceding year (up to ½ amount invested between 6 April and 5 October)	From 2006–07 1998–99 to 2005–06	£50,000 £25,000
Rate of relief	From 1993–94	20%*

* Given as a deduction against income tax liability.

Other reliefs (TCGA ss 150A–150D, Schs 5B, 5BA)
(a) A gain on a disposal of shares on which EIS relief has been given and not withdrawn is exempt from capital gains tax.
(b) Deferral relief is available for gains on assets where the disposal proceeds are reinvested in eligible shares in a qualifying company one year before or three years after the disposal.
(c) A loss on a disposal of shares on which EIS relief has been given may be relieved against income tax or capital gains tax.

Venture capital trusts
(TA 1998 ss 332A, 842AA, Sch 15B, Sch 28B; FA 2002, s 109, Sch 33; FA 2004 s 94, Sch 19; ITTOIA 2005 ss 709–712; FA 2006 s 91, Sch 14)
An individual who subscribes for ordinary shares in a VCT obtains income tax reliefs at the rates in the table below subject to conditions. The shares must be held for at least 5 years (3 years for shares issued before 6 April 2006 and 5 years for shares issued before 6 April 2000).

Relief on investment

Maximum annual investment:	From 2004–05 1995–96 to 2003–04	£200,000 £100,000
Rate of relief:	2006–07 2004–05 to 2005–06 1995–96 to 2003–04	30% 40% 20%

Other reliefs
(a) Dividends on shares within investment limit exempt from income tax (unless the investor's main purpose is tax avoidance – from 9 March 1999).
(b) Capital gains reliefs (see p 28).

Urban Regeneration Companies
Relief is available from 1 April 2003 for expenditure incurred by businesses in making contributions to designated Urban Regeneration Companies (TA 1988 s 79B; FA 2003 s 180; ITTOIA 2005 ss 82, 86).

Investment reliefs — continued

Individual investment plans ('ISAs')

(TA 1988 s 333; ITTOIA 2005 ss 694–701; SI 1998/1870; SI 2001/908)
Savers can subscribe to an ISA up to the following limits per tax year.

Overall annual subscription limit	1999–2000 to 2009–10	£7,000
Cash limit	1999–2000 to 2009–10	£3,000
Life insurance limit	1999–2000 to 2004–05	£1,000

A limit of £3,000 also applies to stocks and shares held in a mini-ISA. The limits are not affected by any TESSAs or PEPs held. The subscription limit applies to each spouse. Shares acquired under an approved share incentive plan, profit sharing scheme or SAYE option scheme may be transferred to a stocks and shares component of an ISA within 90 days without tax consequences.

Reliefs

(a) Investments under the scheme are free from income tax and capital gains tax.
(b) 10% tax credit paid until 5 April 2004 on dividends from UK equities.
(c) Withdrawals may be made at any time without loss of tax relief.

Tax-exempt special savings accounts ('TESSAs')

(Accounts opened **before 6 April 1999**: TA 1988 ss 326A–326C)
Interest and bonuses received in the first five years (or on death if earlier) are exempt from income tax providing conditions are met. Withdrawals within the initial five-year period result in the loss of all tax exemption (including on interest already received). Interest earned after the maturity of the TESSA is taxable. Deposits could be made up to £3,000 in the first 12 months, £1,800 in any succeeding 12-month period and £9,000 in total.

Up to the full amount of the capital at maturity of a first TESSA could be invested in a follow-up TESSA within six months and similar conditions apply to a follow-up TESSA.

The capital in a TESSA opened before 6 April 1999 could, on maturity, be transferred to an ISA (see above). The capital in a TESSA that matured between 6 January 1999 and 5 April 1999 could be transferred into an ISA after 5 April 1999 if no follow-up TESSA was opened. Such transfers do not affect amounts which can be subscribed to an ISA.

Personal equity plans ('PEPs')

(Subscriptions made **before 6 April 1999**: TA 1988 s 333; SI 1989/469; SI 1998/1869)
Before 6 April 1999, subscriptions to PEPs could be made up to a maximum per year of £6,000 to a general plan and £3,000 to a single company plan. Dividend income is tax free and a 10% tax credit was payable until 5 April 2004 on dividends from UK equities. Interest on cash held is paid gross and is tax free if reinvested.

PEPs held at 5 April 1999 can continue to be held with the same tax advantages as an ISA (see above) and without affecting the amount that can be subscribed to an ISA.

National Savings Bank interest

The first £70 of any interest you receive from a National Savings Ordinary Account is tax free. It is not possible to open a new Ordinary Account after 28 January 2004.

Miscellaneous reliefs

Foster carers
(ITTOIA 2005 ss 803–828)
Generally, local authority payments to foster carers are not taxable to the extent they do no more than meet the actual costs of caring. In other cases, for 2003–04 onwards:
- where gross receipts do not exceed the 'individual limit', the carer is treated as having a nil profit and nil loss for the tax year concerned;
- where gross receipts exceed the 'individual limit', the carer can choose to either be taxed on the excess or compute profit or loss using the normal business rules.

The 'individual limit' is made up of a fixed amount of £10,000 per residence for a full tax year plus an amount per child for each week or part week that the individual provides foster care. The weekly amounts are £200 for a child under 11 years and £250 for a child of 11 or over.

Landlord's energy-saving allowance
(ITTOIA 2005 s 312–314)

From 6 April 2004 to 5 April 2009 individual landlords who let residential property and pay income tax may claim a deduction from the property business profits for expenditure in the dwelling houses let to install:
- loft insulation or cavity wall insulation; or
- (from 7 April 2005) solid wall insulation; or
- (from 6 April 2006) draught-proofing and insulation for hot water systems.

Expenditure is restricted to £1,500 per building.

Life assurance premium relief
(TA 1988 s 266, Sch 14 para 7)
Relief for premiums paid on qualifying life assurance policies for contracts made before 14 March 1984 is available by deduction of 12.5% from admissible premiums.

Maintenance payments
(ITTOIA 2005 ss 727, 729; TA 1988 ss 347A, 347B)
Where either party to the marriage was born before 6 April 1935, relief for maintenance payments is given under the rules for arrangements made after 15 March 1988 even if the obligation existed on or before that date. Under these rules the payer can claim tax relief in respect of the lower of:
- the amount of the payments in the year concerned and
- the minimum amount of the married couple's allowance for the year concerned (see p 46).

The relief is restricted to 10% of the relevant amount. The payment must be made to the divorced or separated spouse. It is made gross and is not taxable in the hands of the recipient.

Rent-a-room relief
(ITTOIA 2005 ss 784–802; F(No 2)A 1982 Sch 10)
Gross annual receipts from letting furnished accommodation in the only or main home are exempt from tax up to a maximum of £4,250 (provided no other taxable income is derived from a trade, letting or arrangement from which the rent-a-room receipts are derived).

If the gross receipts exceed £4,250, the taxpayer can pay tax on the net receipts after deduction of expenses. Alternatively, the taxpayer can elect to pay tax on the amount by which the gross receipts exceed £4,250, without relief for the actual expenses.

An individual's maximum is halved to £2,125 if during the 'relevant period' for the year (normally the tax year) some other person received income from letting accommodation in that property.

An election can be made to disapply the relief for a particular tax year (for example, if the individual would otherwise make an allowable loss).

Pension provision from 6 April 2006

(FA 2004 ss 149–284, Schs 28–36)
From 6 April 2006, a new pension scheme tax regime fully replaces pre-existing rules for occupational pension schemes, personal (and stakeholder) pension schemes and retirement annuity schemes.

Tax relief on contributions

Individual contributions: Contributions to registered schemes are not limited by reference to a fraction of earnings and there is no earnings cap. There is no provision for the carry-back or carry-forward of contributions to tax years other than the year of payment.

An individual may make unlimited contributions and tax relief is available on contributions up to the higher of:
- the full amount of relevant earnings; or
- £3,600 provided the scheme operates tax relief at source.

Employer contributions: Employer contributions to registered schemes are deductible for tax purposes, with statutory provision for spreading abnormally large contributions over a period of up to four years. The contributions are not treated as taxable income of the employee.

Annual allowance

Each individual has an annual allowance as set out in the table below. If the annual increase in an individual's rights under all registered schemes exceeds the annual allowance, the excess is chargeable at 40%, the individual being liable for the tax.

	£
Annual allowance 2006–07	215,000[1]

[1] The allowance is set to rise to £255,000 by 2010.

Taxable benefits

'Tax-free' lump sum: The maximum 'tax-free' lump sum that can be paid to a member under a registered scheme is broadly the lower of
- 25% of the value of the pension rights; and
- 25% of the member's lifetime allowance.

Lifetime allowance: Each individual has a lifetime allowance for contributions as set out in the table below. The excess over the lifetime allowance of the benefits crystallising (usually when a pension begins to be paid) is taxable at the following rates:
- at 55% if taken as a lump sum
- at 25% in other cases

Any tax due may be deducted from the individual's benefits.

	£
Lifetime allowance 2006–07	1,500,000[2]

[2] The allowance is set to rise to £1,800,000 by 2010.

Transitional. There are transitional provisions for the protection of lump sum and other pension rights accrued before 6 April 2006.

Age restrictions

Minimum pension age: The minimum pension age is 50 (rising to 55 on 6 April 2010). A pension cannot be paid before the minimum age except on grounds of ill health. Those with existing contractual rights to draw a pension earlier will have those rights protected and there is special protection for members of pre-6 April 2006 approved schemes with early retirement ages (see p 64). A reduced lifetime allowance will apply in the case of early retirement before age 50 except in the case of certain professions such as the police and the armed forces (to be prescribed by regulations).

Maximum benefit age: Benefits must be taken by the age of 75 at the latest. A member of a money purchase scheme may take a pension from the age of 75 by way of income withdrawal (known as an 'alternatively secured pension') instead of taking a scheme pension or purchasing a lifetime annuity. The maximum alternatively secured pension is 70% of a comparable annuity.

Personal pension schemes and retirement annuities

Provisions to 5 April 2006

1 July 1988 to 5 April 2006: Retirement annuity contracts were replaced by personal pension schemes, although retirement annuity premiums may continue to be paid, and tax relief obtained (TA 1988 ss 618–629). There are provisions for the carrying back (TA 1988 s 619) and the carrying forward (TA 1988 s 625) of relief, and these are not affected by FA 2000.

6 April 2001 to 5 April 2006: The personal pension scheme rules were adapted to accommodate the stakeholder pensions provisions (TA 1988 ss 630–655). From that date, personal pension and stakeholder pension contributions are subject to the same rules.

Tax relief on contributions

Retirement annuities: Premiums continue to be deducted from or set off against relevant earnings (TA 1988 s 619). The amount of relief available is based on a percentage of net relevant earnings (see maximum amount, below).

Personal pension schemes: Before 6 April 2001, premiums were deducted from or set off against relevant earnings (TA 1988 s 639, as enacted). The amount of relief available was based on a percentage of net relevant earnings (see maximum amount, below).

Personal pension schemes/stakeholder pensions:

Contributions not exceeding the earnings threshold

(1) Contributions of up to £3,600 gross ('the earnings threshold') may be paid into a stakeholder pension by anyone who is not a member of an occupational pension scheme, regardless of the amount (if any) of their earnings (TA 1988 s 632A).
(2) An individual who is a member of an occupational pension scheme but who is not a controlling director and whose total annual remuneration is no more than £30,000 is allowed to pay into both an occupational scheme and a stakeholder pension and will receive tax relief on an annual contribution of up to £3,600 (gross) into the stakeholder pension (TA 1988 s 632B).

Contributions exceeding the earnings threshold

(1) Contributions in excess of the earnings threshold may be made. Tax relief is given on contributions up to a maximum based on a percentage of net relevant earnings (see maximum percentage below).
(2) For the purpose of supporting contributions in excess of the earnings threshold, a tax year for which evidence of relevant earnings can be provided may be nominated as the basis year and contributions based on the amount of those earnings may be paid in each of the next 5 years (TA 1988 s 646B). The provisions enable an individual to make pension contributions for up to 5 years after the relevant earnings ceased, by reference to the net relevant earnings of a basis year which may be any one of the 6 tax years preceding the first year for which there are no relevant earnings (TA 1988 s 646D).

Carry-back of relief

Carry-back of relief is provided for in TA 1988 s 641A. There is no carry forward of relief (FA 2000 Sch 13 para 19).

Basic and higher rate relief

From 6 April 2001, contributions are payable net of basic rate tax relief. Tax relief at the higher rate is given by extending the basic rate band by the amount of the contribution paid in the year of assessment (TA 1988 s 639).

From 2001–02, relief for contributions is given up to a maximum which is the greater of:
(a) the 'earnings threshold'; and
(b) the 'maximum percentage' of net relevant earnings for the year

(TA 1988 s 640, as amended by FA 2000 Sch 13 para 16). For the purposes of calculating the maximum percentage, net relevant earnings are subject to an earnings cap (TA 1988 s 640A).

Maximum amount

Personal pension schemes/ stakeholder pensions (TA 1988 s 640)		
	Age in years at beginning of year of assessment	Maximum percentage
	35 and below	17½
	36 to 45	20
	46 to 50	25
	51 to 55	30
	56 to 60	35
	61 or more	40
Earnings cap	£	
2005–06	105,600	
2004–05	102,000	
2003–04	99,000	
2002–03	97,200	
2001–02	95,400	
2000–01	91,800	

Personal pension schemes, stakeholder pensions and retirement annuities — continued

Retirement annuities (TA 1988 s 626)		
	Age in years at beginning of year of assessment	Maximum percentage
	50 and below	17½
	51 to 55	20
	56 to 60	22½
	61 or more	27½

Life insurance element (TA 1988 s 640(3), as amended)

The maximum amount of contributions in respect of life insurance on which tax relief can be given is limited to a percentage of net relevant earnings (retirement annuities; personal pension contracts taken out before 6 April 2001) or of total amount of relevant pension contributions (personal pensions/stakeholder pension contracts taken out after 5 April 2001).

	Maximum percentage of net relevant earnings
Retirement annuities (contracts for dependants or life insurance)	5%
Personal pension schemes (contract of life insurance made before 6 April 2001)	5%
	Maximum percentage of total relevant pension contributions
Personal pension schemes/stakeholder pensions Contract of life insurance made after 5 April 2001	10%

Approval of contracts – early retirement ages

Trades and professions for which an early retirement age was agreed by the Revenue under TA 1988 s 620(4)(c) for the purpose of the approval of retirement annuity contracts are set out below. Under the personal and stakeholder pensions legislation, individuals may not take benefits from their pension arrangements before the age of 50. The trades and professions listed below for which the Revenue has approved an earlier retirement age of 30, 35, 40 or 45 have been approved under TA 1988 s 634(3)(b) for the purposes of personal pension schemes and stakeholder pensions. (See p 62 for minimum age restrictions.)

Retirement age	Profession or occupation		
30	downhill skiers		
35	athletes	ice hockey players	table tennis players
	badminton players	models	tennis players (including real tennis players)
	boxers	national hunt jockeys	
	cyclists	rugby league players	wrestlers
	dancers	rugby union players	
	footballers	squash players	
40	cricketers	golfers	speedway drivers
	divers (saturation, deep sea and free swimming)	motorcycle riders (motorcross or road racing)	trapeze artists
		motor racing drivers	WPBSA snooker players
45	flat racing jockeys	members of the reserve forces	
50	circus animal trainers	off-shore riggers (mechanical fitters, pipe fitters, riggers, platers, welders and roustabouts)	rugby league referees
	croupiers		territorial army members
	interdealer brokers		TV newsreaders
	martial arts instructors	Royal Navy reservists	
	moneybroker dealers		
55	air pilots	inshore fishermen	psychiatrists (who are also maximum part-time specialists employed within the NHS solely in the treatment of the mentally disordered)
	brass instrumentalists	midwives (female)	
	distant water trawlermen	moneybroker dealer managers and directors responsible for dealers	
	firemen (part-time)		
	health visitors (female)	nurses (female)	singers
		physiotherapists (female)	

Share schemes

Share incentive plans ('SIPs')
(TCGA 1992 ss 236A, 238A, Schs 7C, 7D Pt 1; ITEPA 2003 ss 488–515, Sch 2; FA 2003 s 139, Sch 21)
Applications for approval of Share Incentive Plans could be made from 28 July 2000.

Free share plan

2000–01 onwards	annual maximum	£3,000

Partnership share plan

2000–01 to 2002–03	monthly maximum	£125 or 10% of monthly salary if lower
2003–04 onwards	annual maximum	£1,500 or 10% of annual salary if lower

Matching shares

2000–01 onwards	Maximum number of shares given by employer to employee for each partnership share bought	2

Shares are free of tax and NICs if held in the plan for five years. Dividends up to £1,500 per employee per tax year are tax free if reinvested in shares. Shares withdrawn from the plan at any time are exempt from capital gains tax and are treated as acquired by the employee at their market value at that time.

If shares are withdrawn within between three and five years (with exceptions such as on death, disability, normal retirement or redundancy), liability to income tax and NICs arises on the lower of their value on entering and on leaving the plan. If shares are withdrawn within three years (with similar exceptions), liability is on their value on leaving the plan.

Enterprise management incentives
(TCGA 1992 s 238A, Sch 7D Pt 4; ITEPA 2003 ss 527–541, Sch 5)

With effect from 28 July 2000, certain independent trading companies with gross assets not exceeding £15 million may grant share options then worth up to £100,000 to an eligible employee. The total value of shares in respect of which unexercised qualifying options exist must not exceed £3 million. (For options granted before 11 May 2001 the number of employees who could hold options at any one time was limited to 15, giving an overall limit of £1·5 million.)

Where the conditions of the scheme are complied with –
  (a) There is no charge to tax or NICs when the option is granted provided the option to acquire the shares is not at less than their market values at that date, and there is no charge on exercise providing the option is exercised within ten years.
  (b) Capital gains tax will be payable when the shares are sold, but business assets taper relief (see p 26) will be available and starts from the date on which the options are granted.

Approved save as you earn (SAYE) share option schemes
(TCGA 1992 s 238A, Sch 7D Pt 2; ITEPA 2003 ss 516–520, Sch 3; FA 2003 s 139, Sch 21)

The scheme is linked to an approved savings scheme, on which bonuses are exempt from tax, to provide funds for the acquisition of shares when the option is exercised at the end of a 3 or 5-year contract. A 5-year contract may offer the option of repayment on the 7th anniversary.

Monthly contributions to SAYE scheme

Minimum	£5–£10[1]
Maximum	£250

[1] The company may choose a minimum savings contribution between £5 and £10.
See the Treasury website (www.hm-treasury.gov.uk) for the bonus rates.

Where the conditions of the scheme are complied with, no income tax charge arises on the employee in respect of –
  (a) the grant of an option to acquire shares at a discount of up to 20% of the share price at time of the grant;
  (b) the exercise of the option (options must not be exercised before the bonus date subject to cessation of employment due to injury, disability, redundancy, retirement or death); or
  (c) any increase in the value of the shares.

Capital gains tax is chargeable on disposal of the shares: the CGT base cost is the consideration given by the employee for both the shares and the option.

Share schemes — continued

Company share option plans ('CSOPs')
(TCGA 1992 s 238A, Sch 7D Pt 3; ITEPA 2003 ss 521–526, Sch 4; FA 2003 s 139, Sch 21)

Limit on value of shares under option held by employee at any one time

From 29 April 1996	£30,000

Scheme shares must be fully paid up, not redeemable and not subject to special restrictions. Only full-time directors or qualifying employees may participate in the scheme.

Where the conditions of the scheme are complied with, no tax charge arises on the employee in respect of –
- (a) the grant of an option to acquire shares[1];
- (b) the exercise of the option[2]; or
- (c) any increase in the value of the shares.

Capital gains tax is chargeable on disposal of the shares: the CGT base cost is the consideration given by the employee for both the shares and the option.

[1] At the time the option is granted the price at which shares can be acquired must not be less than the market value of shares of the same class at that time.
[2] The option must be exercised between 3 and 10 years after the grant (or may be exercised less than 3 years after the grant where the individual ceases to be an employee due to injury, disablement, redundancy or retirement). For options granted before 9 April 2003, the options must be exercised between 3 and 10 years after the grant (without exception) and not less than 3 years after a previous exempt exercise of another option under the same or another approved company share option scheme.

Approved profit sharing schemes
(TA 1988 ss 186, 187, Schs 9, 10)

NOTE: The income tax relief in respect of awards of shares under approved profit sharing schemes was withdrawn for awards of shares made after 31 December 2002: FA 2000 s 49.

Annual limit on shares appropriated

From 1991–92	Greater of £3,000 or 10% of salary, up to £8,000

Schedule E charge on early disposal or receipt of capital from shares

Time of disposal or capital receipt	Percentage charge[1]
Before 3rd anniversary of appropriation	100%[2]

[1] Calculated on the appropriate percentage of the initial market value of the shares when appropriated (or the sales proceeds if less).
[2] The charge is reduced to 50% where the employee reaches the retirement age specified in the scheme rules or leaves the employment due to injury, disability or redundancy before the shares are sold or capital is received.

Where the conditions of the scheme are satisfied, no tax charge arises on the employee in respect of –
- (a) the value of the shares at the time of appropriation;
- (b) any increase in the value of the shares; or
- (c) any gain on the disposal of the shares (although capital gains tax is chargeable on any gain over the market value on appropriation).

Approved discretionary ('executive') share option schemes
Options held on 17 July 1995: (TA 1988 ss 185, 187, Sch 9)

Shares could be acquired at discount of up to 15% of market value at the time of the grant where the employer also had an approved profit sharing scheme or an approved SAYE option scheme. No tax charge arose when the option was granted unless the price paid for the option plus the price at which the shares could be acquired was less than the market value of the shares, in which case, the discount was chargeable. In all other material respects, the rules are the same as for the CSOP schemes (see above).

The scheme was abolished for options granted after 16 July 1995.

Tax credits

From 6 April 2003, child tax credit ('CTC') and working tax credit ('WTC') replaced children's tax credit, working families tax credit and disabled person's tax credit in addition to the child-related elements of certain other social security benefits. They are administered and paid by HMRC and are non-taxable. Claims must be made after the commencement of the tax year and can be backdated for a maximum of three months.

Child tax credit and working tax credit

	2006–07 Annual amount	2005–06 Annual amount
Child tax credit	£	£
Family element[1]	545	545
Addition for child under age of 1[1]	545	545
Child element (for each child or young person)	1,765	1,690
Addition for disabled child or young person	2,350	2,285
Enhancement for severe disabled child or young person	945	920
Working tax credit	£	£
Basic element	1,665	1,620
Lone parent and couple element	1,640	1,595
30-hour element	680	660
Disability element	2,225	2,165
Severe disability element	945	920
50+ element—16 to 29 hours worked	1,140	1,110
50+ element—30 or more hours worked[2]	1,705	1,660
Childcare element (up to 80% (70% for 2005/06) of eligible costs)	**Weekly**	**Weekly**
—maximum eligible cost for 1 child	175.00	175.00
—maximum eligible cost for 2 or more children	300.00	300.00

Income thresholds and withdrawal rates	2006–07	2005–06
First income threshold for those entitled to CTC amd WTC	£5,220	£5,220
First withdrawal rate	37%	37%
Second income threshold	£50,000	£50,000
Second withdrawal rate	6.67%	6.67%
First threshold for those entitled to CTC only	£14,155	£13,910
Income disregarded	£25,000	£2,500

[1] Only one family element available per family. The baby element is payable in addition in the first year of the child's life.
[2] Where an individual qualifies for the 50 plus (30+ hours) payment, they cannot also qualify for the 50 plus (16–29 hours) payment.

Calculation of award. Tax credits are awarded on an annual basis. They are initially based on the income of the claimant or joint claimants for the preceding tax year and then adjusted based on actual income in the tax year in which the credit is claimed.

Income broadly includes all taxable income excluding the first £300 of income from pensions, savings, property or foreign assets. If actual income is greater than the previous year's income by less than £25,000, the award is not adjusted. If actual income is less than the previous year's income or if it is greater than the previous year's income by £25,000 or more (£2,500 before April 2006), the award is adjusted to reflect actual income.

Where annual income exceeds the first income threshold, the excess is tapered (by 37%) and the balance deducted from the maximum tax credit entitlement. However, the family element of CTC is not reduced until income exceeds the second income threshold at which point the excess is tapered at 6.67%. The taper applies in order to the WTC elements, the WTC childcare elements, the CTC child elements and the CTC family elements.

Where circumstances change during a tax year and different rates apply, the award is recalculated on a proportional, daily basis. Such changes must be notified to HMRC within three months if tax credit entitlement will be reduced as a result. From April 2007, this time limit is to be reduced to one month.

Eligibility. CTC is payable to UK resident single parents and couples responsible for a child or young person.

WTC is payable to UK residents who are at least 16 years old and who work (or in the case of a couple, one of whom works) at least 16 hours a week. Additionally, the claimant (or one of them if a couple) must either:

- be at least 25 years old and work at least 30 hours a week; or
- have a dependent child or children; or
- be over 50 and qualify for the 50+ element; or
- have a mental or physical disability which puts them at a disadvantage in getting a job and have previously been in receipt of some form of disability benefit.

Renewal claim. Claims for tax credit must be renewed by 31 August. Before 2006–07 the renewal date was 30 September.

Inheritance tax

Rates of tax

From 15 March 1988 onwards

Cumulative gross transfer rate:	Rate
for gross transfers on death over the cumulative chargeable transfer limit	40%
for gross lifetime transfers over the cumulative chargeable transfer limit	20%
Grossing-up net transfer rate for each £1 over the chargeable transfer limit:	
for net transfers on death not bearing own tax	2/3
for net lifetime transfers	1/4

Cumulative chargeable transfer limits

Period	Limit £	Period	Limit £
2009–10[1]	325,000	1999–2000	231,000
2008–09[1]	312,000	1998–99	223,000
2007–08[2]	300,000	1997–98	215,000
2006–07	285,000	1996–97	200,000
2005–06	275,000	1995–96	154,000
2004–05	263,000	10.3.92–5.4.95	150,000
2003–04	255,000	6.4.91–9.3.92	140,000
2002–03	250,000	1990–91	128,000
2001–02	242,000	1989–90	118,000
2000–01	234,000		

Notes
[1] FA 2006 s 155.
[2] FA 2005 s 98.

Delivery of accounts: due dates

Type of transfer	Due date
Chargeable lifetime transfers	Later of – (a) 12 months after the end of the month in which the transfer took place; and (b) 3 months after the date on which the person delivering the account became liable
PETs which become chargeable	12 months after the end of the month in which the transferor died
Gifts with reservation chargeable on death	12 months after the end of the month in which the death occurred
Transfers on death	Later of – (a) 12 months after the end of the month in which the death occurred; and (b) 3 months after the date on which the personal representatives first act or the person liable first has reason to believe that he is liable to deliver an account
National heritage property	6 months after the end of the month in which the chargeable event occurred

Delivery of accounts: excepted transfers and estates
(SI 2002 No 1733, SI 2004 No 2543)

Date of transfer or death	6 April 2000–5 April 2002	6 April 2002–5 April 2003	6 April 2003–31 Aug 2006	From 1 Sept 2006
	Value below	Value below	Value below	Value below
Excepted transfers:				
Total chargeable transfers since 6 April	£10,000	£10,000	£10,000	£10,000
Total chargeable transfers during last 10 years	£40,000	£40,000	£40,000	£40,000
Excepted estates:				
Total gross value	£210,000[1]	£220,000[1]	£240,000[1] (see (a) below)	(see (a) below)
Total gross value of property outside UK	£50,000	£75,000	£75,000	£100,000
Aggregate value of 'specified transfers'[2]	£75,000	£100,000	£100,000	£150,000
Settled property passing on death	—	£100,000	£100,000	£150,000

Excepted estates
For deaths occurring after 5 April 2004, no account need be delivered where the deceased died domiciled in the UK provided either conditions (a) or (b) below are met, and both conditions (c) and (d) below are met.
(a) the aggregate of the gross value of the estate, and of any 'specified transfers' or 'specified exempt transfers'[3] does not exceed the appropriate IHT threshold;
(b) the aggregate of the gross value of the estate, and of any 'specified transfers' or 'specified exempt transfers'[3] does not exceed £1,000,000; and after deducting from that aggregate figure any exempt spouse and charity transfers and total estate liabilities, it does not exceed the appropriate IHT threshold;
(c) the gross value of settled property or foreign assets do not exceed the above limits; and
(d) there were no chargeable lifetime transfers in the 7 years before death other than specified transfers not exceeding the above limits.

For deaths occurring after 31 August 2006, an estate will not be an excepted estate if the provisions for alternatively secured pension funds in IHTA 1984 ss 151A–151C apply by reason of the individual's death.

For deaths after 5 April 2002 and before 6 April 2004, no account need be delivered where the deceased died domiciled in the UK provided that:
(i) the aggregate of the gross value of the estate, and of any 'specified transfers' does not exceed the above limits; and
(ii) the gross value of settled property or foreign assets do not exceed the above limits; and
(iii) there were no chargeable lifetime transfers in the 7 years before death other than specified transfers not exceeding the above limits.

Where the deceased was never domiciled in the UK, no account need be delivered for deaths after 5 April 2002 provided that:
- the value of the estate in the UK is wholly attributable to cash and quoted shares and securities not exceeding £150,000 (£100,000 before 1 September 2006); and
- for deaths occurring after 31 August 2006, the provisions for alternatively secured pension funds in IHTA 1984 ss 151A–151C do not apply by reason of the individual's death.

Notes
[1] This limit applies to the aggregate gross value of the estate and of 'specified transfers'[3].
[2] 'Specified transfers' are transfers of cash, quoted shares and securities and, after 6 April 2002, interests in or over land and, after 5 April 2004, personal chattels or corporeal moveable property.
[3] 'Specified exempt transfers' are transfers in the 7 years before death between spouses, gifts to charity, political parties or housing associations, transfers to maintenance funds for historical buildings, etc. or to employee trusts.

Excepted settlements
No account need be delivered of property comprised in excepted settlements where a chargeable event occurs after 5 April 2002. An 'excepted settlement' is one comprising solely of cash not exceeding £1,000 and in which there is no interest in possession. The trustees must be UK resident throughout the life of the trust and there must be no related settlements.

Inheritance tax — continued

Reliefs

The following is a summary of the main reliefs and exemptions under the Inheritance Tax Act 1984. The legislation should be referred to for conditions and exceptions.

Agricultural property
Transfer with vacant possession (or right to obtain it within 12 months); transfer on or after 1 September 1995, of land let (or treated as let) on or after that date.   100% of agricultural value
Any other case   50% of agricultural value

Note: The 100% relief is extended in limited circumstances by Concession F17.

Annual gifts   £3,000

Business property

Unincorporated business Unquoted shares (including shares in AIM or USM companies) (held for 2 years or more)[1] Unquoted securities which alone, or together with other such securities and unquoted shares, give the transferor control of the company (held for 2 years or more)[1] Settled property used in life tenant's business	100%	Controlling holding in fully quoted companies Land, buildings, machinery or plant used in business of company or partnership 50%

[1] Tax charges arising and transfers occurring after 5 April 1996. 10 March 1992–5 April 1996 minority holding of shares or securities of up to 25% in unquoted or USM company qualified for 50% relief; larger holdings qualified for 100% relief.

Charities, gifts to   Exempt
From 1 April 2002, Community Amateur Sports Clubs are treated as charities

Marriage gifts
Made by: parent   £5,000
          remoter ancestor   £2,500
          party to marriage   £2,500
          other person   £1,000

National purposes
Property given or bequeathed to bodies listed in IHTA 1984 Sch 3   Exempt

Political parties, gifts to   Exempt

Potentially exempt transfers
Exempt if made 7 or more years before the date of death. Except for gifts with reservation etc, they include:
(a) transfers by individuals to other individuals or certain trusts for the disabled;
(b) transfers after 21 March 2006 by individuals to a bereaved minor's trust on the coming to an end of an immediate post-death interest;
(c) transfers before 22 March 2006 by individuals to accumulation and maintenance trusts;
(d) transfers by individuals into interest in possession trusts in which, for transfers after 21 March 2006, the beneficiary has a disabled person's interest; and
(e) certain transfers on the termination or disposal of an individual's beneficial interest in possession in settled property (in restricted circumstances following FA 2006).

Quick succession relief
Estate increased by chargeable transfer followed by death within 5 years
Death within first year   100%
Each additional year: decreased by   20%

Small gifts to same person   £250

Spouses with separate domicile (one not being in the UK)
Total exemption   £55,000

Tapering relief
The value of the estate on death is taxed as the top slice of cumulative transfers in the 7 years before death. Transfers on or within 7 years of death are taxed on their value at the date of the gift on the death rate scale, but using the scale in force at the date of death, subject to the following taper—

Years between gift and death	Percentage of full charge at death rates
0–3	100
3–4	80
4–5	60
5–6	40
6–7	20

Penalties see p 12.

National insurance contributions

From 6 April 2006

Class 1 contributions[1]				
Earnings limits and threshold		Weekly £	Monthly £	Yearly £
Lower earnings limit		84	364	4,368
Earnings threshold		97	420	5,035
Upper earnings limit		645	2,795	33,540

Not contracted out		Employees' contributions	Employers' contributions	
Weekly earnings:	£97.01–£645	11%	12.8%	
	Over £645	1%	12.8%	

Contracted out			Salary-related schemes	Money purchase schemes
Weekly earnings:	£97.01–£645	9.4%	9.3%	11.8%
	Over £645	1%	12.8%	12.8%
	—rebate £84–£97	1.6%[2]	3.5%	1%

Women at reduced rate				
Weekly earnings:	£97.01–£645	4.85%	as above	
	Over £645	1%	as above	

Class 1A and Class 1B contributions		12.8%

Class 2 (self-employed)	Flat rate	£2.10 a week
	Share fishermen	£2.75 a week
	Volunteer development workers	£4.20 a week
	Small earnings exception	£4,465 a year

Class 3 (voluntary contributions)		£7.55 a week

Class 4 (self-employed)[3]	annual profits:	£5,035–£33,540	8%
		Over £33,540	1%

Maximum contributions
Class 1 or Class 1/Class 2[4]   £3,194.84 plus 1% of earnings over the upper earnings limit
Class 4 limiting amount[5]   £2,391.70 plus 1% of profits over £33,540 a year

Notes:
[1] Employees' rates are nil for children under 16, men over 65 and women over 60 but employers' contributions are still payable. NICs are not payable on earnings up to the earnings threshold.
[2] The rebate is given on earnings between the lower earnings limit and the earnings threshold. The rebate for employees is given to employers to the extent that insufficient contributions have been paid by the employee for offset.
[3] Not payable if pensionable age is reached by the beginning of the tax year.
[4] Where an earner has more than one employment (including self-employment), liability for Class 1 or Class 1 and Class 2 contributions cannot exceed a maximum amount equal to 53 employees' Class 1 contributions at the maximum standard rate, plus, from 2003–04 onwards, 1% on earnings over the individual's upper earnings limit (which varies depending on individual circumstances).
[5] Where Class 4 contributions are payable in addition to Class 1 and/or Class 2 contributions, liability for Class 4 contributions cannot exceed such an amount as, when added to the Class 1/Class 2 contributions payable (after applying the maximum if appropriate), equals the limiting amount. The limiting amount is the maximum Class 4 contributions payable (including, from 2003–04 onwards, 1% on earnings over the upper profit limit) plus 53 Class 2 contributions.

National insurance contributions — continued

6 April 2005–5 April 2006

Class 1 contributions[1]			
Lower earnings limit	£82 a week	£356 a month	£4,264 a year
Earnings threshold	£94 a week	£408 a month	£4,895 a year
Upper earnings limit	£630 a week	£2,730 a month	£32,760 a year

Not contracted out		Employees' contributions	Employers' contributions	
Weekly earnings:	£94.01–£630	11%	12.8%	
	Over £630	1%	12.8%	

Contracted out			Salary-related schemes	Money purchase schemes
Weekly earnings:	£94.01–£630	9.4%	9.3%	11.8%
	Over £630	1%	12.8%	12.8%
	—rebate £82–£94	1.6%[2]	3.5%	1%

Women at reduced rate				
Weekly earnings:	£94.01–£630	4.85%	as above	
	Over £630	1%	as above	

Class 1A and Class 1B contributions		12.8%

Class 2 (self-employed)	Flat rate	£2.10 a week
	Share fishermen	£2.75 a week
	Volunteer development workers	£4.10 a week
	Small earnings exception	£4,345 a year

Class 3 (voluntary contributions)	£7.35 a week

Class 4 (self-employed)[3]	annual profits £4,895–£32,760: 8% plus 1% of profits over £32,760

Maximum contributions	
Class 1 or Class 1/Class 2[4]	£3,124.88 plus 1% of earnings over the upper earnings limit
Class 4 limiting amount[5]	£2,340.50 plus 1% of profits over £32,760 a year

6 April 2004–5 April 2005

Class 1 contributions[1]			
Lower earnings limit	£79 a week	£343 a month	£4,108 a year
Earnings threshold	£91 a week	£395 a month	£4,745 a year
Upper earnings limit	£610 a week	£2,644 a month	£31,720 a year

Not contracted out		Employees' contributions	Employers' contributions	
Weekly earnings:	£91.01–£610	11%	12.8%	
	Over £610	1%	12.8%	

Contracted out			Salary-related schemes	Money purchase schemes
Weekly earnings:	£91.01–£610	9.4%	9.3%	11.8%
	Over £610	1%	12.8%	12.8%
	—rebate £79–£91	1.6%[2]	3.5%	1%

Women at reduced rate				
Weekly earnings:	£91.01–£610	4.85%	as above	
	Over £610	1%	as above	

Class 1A and Class 1B contributions		12.8%

Class 2 (self-employed)	Flat rate	£2.05 a week
	Share fishermen	£2.70 a week
	Volunteer development workers	£3.95 a week
	Small earnings exception	£4,215 a year

Class 3 (voluntary contributions)	£7.15 a week

Class 4 (self-employed)[3]	annual profits £4,745–£31,720: 8% plus 1% of profits over £31,720

Maximum contributions	
Class 1 or Class 1/Class 2[4]	£3,205.77 plus 1% of earnings over the upper earnings limit
Class 4 limiting amount[5]	£2,266.65 plus 1% of profits over £31,720 a year

See page 71 for notes.

6 April 2003–5 April 2004

Class 1 contributions[1]			
Lower earnings limit	£77 a week	£334 a month	£4,004 a year
Earnings threshold	£89 a week	£385 a month	£4,615 a year
Upper earnings limit	£595 a week	£2,579 a month	£30,940 a year

Not contracted out		Employees' contributions	Employers' contributions	
Weekly earnings:	£89.01–£595	11%	12.8%	
	Over £595	1%	12.8%	

Contracted out			Salary-related schemes	Money purchase schemes
Weekly earnings:	£89.01–£595	9.4%	9.3%	11.8%
	Over £595	1%	12.8%	12.8%
	—rebate £77–£89	1.6%[2]	3.5%	1%

Women at reduced rate				
Weekly earnings:	£89.01–£595	4.85%	as above	
	Over £595	1%	as above	

Class 1A and Class 1B contributions	12.8%

Class 2 (self-employed)	Flat rate	£2 a week
	Share fishermen	£2.65 a week
	Volunteer development workers	£3.85 a week
	Small earnings exception	£4,095 a year

Class 3 (voluntary contributions)	£6.95 a week

Class 4 (self-employed)[3]	annual profits £4,615–£30,940: 8% plus 1% of profits over £30,940

Maximum contributions	
Class 1 or Class 1/Class 2[4]	£2,949.98 plus 1% of earnings over the upper earnings limit
Class 4 limiting amount[5]	£2,212.00 plus 1% of profits over £30,940 a year

6 April 2002–5 April 2003

Class 1 contributions[1]			
Lower earnings limit	£75 a week	£325 a month	£3,900 a year
Earnings threshold	£89 a week	£385 a month	£4,615 a year
Upper earnings limit	£585 a week	£2,535 a month	£30,420 a year

Not contracted out		Employees' contributions	Employers' contributions	
Weekly earnings:	£89.01–£585	10%	11.8%	
	Over £585	no additional liability	11.8%	

Contracted out			Salary-related schemes	Money purchase schemes
Weekly earnings:	£89.01–£585	8.4%	8.3%	10.8%
	Over £585	no additional liability	11.8%	11.8%
	—rebate £75–£89	1.6%[2]	3.5%	1%

Women at reduced rate				
Weekly earnings:	£89.01–£585	3.85%	as above	
	Over £585	no additional liability	as above	

Class 1A and Class 1B contributions	11.8%

Class 2 (self-employed)	Flat rate	£2 a week
	Share fishermen	£2.65 a week
	Volunteer development workers	£3.75 a week
	Small earnings exception	£4,025 a year

Class 3 (voluntary contributions)	£6.85 a week

Class 4 (self-employed)[3]	7% of profits between £4,615–£30,420 a year

Maximum contributions	
Class 1 or Class 1/Class 2[4]	£2,628.80
Class 4 limiting amount[5]	£1,912.35

See page 71 for notes.

National insurance contributions — continued

6 April 2001–5 April 2002

Class 1 contributions[1]
Lower earnings limit	£72 a week	£312 a month	£3,744 a year
Earnings threshold	£87 a week	£378 a month	£4,535 a year
Upper earnings limit	£575 a week	£2,492 a month	£29,900 a year

Not contracted out

		Employees' contributions	Employers' contributions
Weekly earnings:	£87.01–£575	10%	11.9%
	Over £575	no additional liability	11.9%

Contracted out

			Salary-related schemes	Money purchase schemes
Weekly earnings:	£87.01–£575	8.4%	8.9%	11.3%
	Over £575	no additional liability	11.9%	11.9%
	—rebate £72–£87	1.6%[2]	3%	0.6%

Women at reduced rate

Weekly earnings:	£87.01–£575	3.85%	as above	
	Over £575	no additional liability	as above	

Class 1A and Class 1B contributions — 11.9%

Class 2 (self-employed)
- Flat rate — £2 a week
- Share fishermen — £2.65 a week
- Volunteer development workers — £3.60 a week
- Small earnings exception — £3,955 a year

Class 3 (voluntary contributions) — £6.75 a week

Class 4 (self-employed)[3] — 7% of profits between £4,535–£29,900 a year

Maximum contributions
- Class 1 or Class 1/Class 2[4] — £2,586.40
- Class 4 limiting amount[5] — £1,881.55

6 April 2000–5 April 2001

Class 1 contributions[1]
Lower earnings limit	£67 a week	£291 a month	£3,484 a year
Employees' earnings (primary) threshold	£76 a week	£329 a month	£3,952 a year
Employers' earnings (secondary) threshold	£84 a week	£365 a month	£4,385 a year
Upper earnings limit	£535 a week	£2,319 a month	£27,820 a year

Employees' contributions

		Not contracted out	Contracted out
Weekly earnings:	£76.01–£535	10%	8.4%
	Over £535	no additional liability	no additional liability
	—rebate		1.6%[2]

Employers' contributions

			Salary-related schemes	Money purchase schemes
Weekly earnings:	£84.01–£535	12.2%	9.2%	11.6%
	Over £535	12.2%	12.2%	12.2%
	—rebate		3%	0.6%

Women at reduced rate

Weekly earnings: £76.01–£535 3.85% Over £535 no additional liability
Normal employers' contributions are payable as above

Class 1A and Class 1B contributions 12.2%

Class 2 (self-employed)
- Flat rate — £2 a week
- Share fishermen — £2.65 a week
- Volunteer development workers — £3.35 a week
- Small earnings exception — £3,825 a year

Class 3 (voluntary contributions) — £6.55 a week

Class 4 (self-employed)[3] — 7% of profits between £4,385–£27,820 a year

Maximum contributions
- Class 1 or Class 1/Class 2[4] — £2,432.70
- Class 4 limiting amount[5] — £1,746.45

See page 71 for notes.

Employers' contributions: benefits in kind

Class 1A national insurance contributions are payable by employers on most taxable benefits in kind, excluding benefits:

(1) which are covered by a dispensation;
(2) included in a PAYE settlement agreement;
(3) provided to employees not earning more than £8,500 pa (including benefits in kind and expenses payments);
(4) otherwise not required to be included on a PIID;
(5) on which Class 1 national insurance contributions were due.

Class 1B contributions are payable by employers by reference to the value of any items included in a PAYE settlement agreement (PSA) which would otherwise be earnings for Class 1 or Class 1A, including the amount of tax paid. Income tax and Class 1B contributions on a PSA are payable by 19 October after the end of the tax year to which the PSA relates.

Common benefits subject to Class 1 and Class 1A NICs (CWG5 2006)

Benefit	NICs Class	PAYE or P11D
Assets/gifts given to employees*	1A	P11D
Assets loaned to employees	1A	P11D
Car or van fuel supplied for private motoring	1A	P11D
Cars or vans available for private use	1A	P11D
Car parking other than at or near place of work or as part of business travel*	1A	P11D
Christmas gifts – cash	1	PAYE
– benefits	1A	P11D
Clothing and uniforms		
– cash payment for clothing that can be worn at any time	1	PAYE
– cash payment for clothing that can only be worn at work or non-durable items such as tights or stockings	–	PAYE
– clothing provided by employer that can be worn at any time	1A	P11D
Computers provided for private use where value exceeds £2,500 (all computers provided for private use after 5.4.06)	1A	P11D
Credit cards and tokens – personal expenses not reimbursed	1	P11D
Entertaining – non-business staff expenses/allowances*	1A	P11D
Holidays provided*	1A	P11D
Living accommodation (beneficial)	1A	P11D
Loans – at low interest or interest-free	1A	P11D
– written off	1	P11D
Meals provided other than at canteen or at business premises open to all staff on a reasonable scale	1A	P11D
Medical insurance or treatment provided in the UK by employer	1A	P11D
Notional payments	1	PAYE
Payments in kind convertible to cash	1	PAYE
Payments of employees personal liabilities	1	PAYE
Prize money	1	PAYE
Relocation payments – qualifying over £8,000	1A	P11D
– non-qualifying benefits	1A	P11D
– non-qualifying expenses	1	P11D
Round sum allowances (not identified as business expense)	1	PAYE
Scholarships awarded to students because of parent's employment or payment of school fees*	1A	P11D
Services supplied	1A	P11D
Tax paid for and not reimbursed by employee	1	P11D
Telephone rental and private calls – employer subscribes*	1A	P11D
Vouchers (other than exceptions for childcare, meals, etc)	1	P11D

*Reimbursement of or payment for goods or services for personal use by employee or payment of personal expenses or allowances where the employee contracts with the supplier, is subject to Class 1 NICs and is reportable on form P11D.

Overseas

Average rates of exchange

Average for year ending	31.3.04	31.12.04	31.3.05	31.12.05	31.3.06
Algeria (Dinar)	126·6578	131·4975	132·9205	132·3118	130·3635
Argentina (Peso)	4·881	5·402	5·4508	5·3182	5·2768
Australia ($A)	2·4488	2·4912	2·4986	2·3862	2·37825
Austria (Euro)	1·44	1·474	1·467	1·4626	1·4664
Bahrain (Dinar)	0·6376	0·6917	0·6968	0·6859	0·6729
Bangladesh (Taka)	99·4753	108·9708	111·5317	116·7483	117·237
Barbados (BD$)	3·3697	3·6574	3·6848	3·639	3·57
Belgium (Euro)	1·44	1·474	1·467	1·4626	1·4664
Bolivia (Boliviano)	13·1051	14·5681	14·7661	14·666	14·36
Botswana (Pula)	8·0961	8·562	8·5027	9·2512	9·51
Brazil (Real)	4·9999	5·3511	5·2779	4·4133	4·1126
Brunei ($)	2·9419	3·0908	3·089	3·0182	2·9546
Burma (Kyat)	10·6399	11·779	11·866	11·6811	11·4616
Burundi (Franc)	1,802·3	1,941·2442	1,963·573	1,920·5317	1,839·63
Canada (Can$)	2·2893	2·384	2·3573	2·2063	2·1598
Cayman Islands (CI$)	1·3987	1·5106	1·523	1·501	1·4774
Chile (Peso)	1,102·876	1,116·725	1,118·999	1,018·873	975·9229
China (Renminbi Yuan)	14·0961	15·1577	15·2827	14·8666	14·4759
Colombia (Peso)	4,656·48	4,803·5	4,674·58	4,227·3334	4,107·4241
Congo Dem Rep (Zaire) (Congolese Franc)	719·4719	753·258	797·5428	886·8474	864·3402
Costa Rica (Colon)	699·2543	805·2731	830·7517	869·6228	869·708
Cuba (Peso)	1/4/03–31/12/03 34·8824 1/1/04–31/3/04 1·8289	1·8314	1·8465	1·8162	1·7815
Cyprus (£)	0·8467	0·8572	0·8509	0·8438	0·8417
Czech Republic (Koruna)	46·464	47·0014	45·652	43·66	43·1314
Denmark (Krone)	10·7070	10·9655	10·9121	10·8991	10·93255
Egypt (£)	10·3236	11·3764	11·2929	10·538	10·2955
El Salvador (Colon)	14·9044	16·028	16·1604	15·8952	15·5912
Ethiopia (Birr)	14·5257	15·7273	15·8847	15·7915	15·5295
European Union (Euro)	1·44	1·474	1·467	1·4626	1·4664
Fiji Islands (F$)	3·0813	3·1709	3·1678	3·0678	3·0556
Finland (Euro)	1·44	1·474	1·467	1·4626	1·4664
France (Euro)	1·44	1·474	1·467	1·4626	1·4664
French Cty/Africa (CFA franc)	947·8783	966·9058	960·6808	959·9	961·102
French Pacific Is (CFP franc)	169·7237	175·0749	174·5547	174·5057	174·724
Gambia (Dalasi)	48·429	53·9398	54·2474	51·7924	50·3634
Germany (Euro)	1·44	1·474	1·467	1·4626	1·4664
Ghana (Cedi)	14,825·84	16,488·517	16,679·57	16,513·74	16,225·61
Greece (Euro)	1·44	1·474	1·467	1·4626	1·4664
Grenada/Wind· Isles (EC$)	4·5399	4·9525	4·99	4·9126	4·8195
Guyana (G$)	303·5003	328·4189	330·8431	335·8187	334·5235
Honduras (Lempira)	29·9331	33·3949	34·0669	34·1971	33·6188
Hong Kong (HK$)	13·1806	14·268	14·3762	14·1526	13·9682
Hungary (Forint)	372·2082	369·4715	362·5755	363·5366	367·705
Iceland (Krona)	125·943	128·2386	125·1205	114·2941	113·7708
India (Rupee)	77·7583	82·9188	82·8631	80·099	78·8637
Indonesia (Rupiah)	14,361·3	16,422·433	16,916·541	17,636·33	17,323·1629
Iran (Rial)	14,059·8	15,816·065	16,145·573	16,299·03	16,111·9
Iraq (Dinar)	1/4/03–20/2/04 0·5234 21/2/04–31/3/04 2,187·62	1/1/04–20/2/04 0·5734 21/2/04–31/12/04 2,368·6802	2,697·8116	2,667·384	2,620·743

Average for year ending	31.3.04	31.12.04	31.3.05	31.12.05	31.3.06
Ireland (Rep. of) (Euro)	1·44	1·474	1·467	1·4626	1·4664
Israel (Shekel)	7·5603	8·2138	8·2195	8·1539	8·1412
Italy (Euro)	1·44	1·474	1·467	1·4626	1·4664
Jamaica (J$)	100·3891	111·4187	112·6475	112·8199	112·3691
Japan (Yen)	190·9326	198·065	198·171	200·1041	201·2374
Jordan (Dinar)	1·2188	1·3007	1·3102	1·2893	1·2648
Kenya (Shilling)	128·7432	145·2923	145·9332	137·2843	132·8881
Korea South (Won)	2,017·287	2,084·2033	2,029·15	1,852·275	1,797·1
Kuwait (Dinar)	0·5031	0·5408	0·5435	0·5313	0·5213
Laos (New Kip)	13,154·55	14,397·408	14,498·05	17,674·3833	18,440·6
Lebanon (£)	2,566·365	2,778·0553	2,798·3398	2,744·3486	2,687·5416
Libya (Dinar)	2·1938	2·3891	2·3908	2·3765	2·3642
Luxembourg (Euro)	1·44	1·474	1·467	1·4626	1·4664
Malawi (Kwacha)	171·341	198·5154	200·7741	214·9901	220·5461
Malaysia (Ringgit)	6·4423	6·9715	7·023	6·8872	6·7233
Malta (Lira)	0·6164	0·6306	0·6286	0·6285	0·6293
Mauritius (Rupee)	46·5149	50·5845	52·2987	53·4296	53·3423
Mexico (Peso)	18·385	20·6952	20·9278	19·8317	19·1852
Morocco (Dirham)	15·7817	16·256	16·1825	16·1185	16·0777
Nepal (Rupee)	126·7737	132·5356	132·6487	127·9483	125·954
Netherlands (Euro)	1·44	1·474	1·467	1·4626	1·4664
N'nd Antilles (Guilder)	3·036	3·2781	3·3052	3·251	3·1888
New Zealand (NZ$)	2·7677	2·7591	2·7339	2·5815	2·5841
Nicaragua (Gold Cordoba)	25·9672	29·0374	29·5863	29·7796	29·6126
Nigeria (Naira)	226·7154	246·3451	246·7575	241·7492	235·493
Norway (Krone)	11·9099	12·347	12·1438	11·7178	11·6878
Oman (Rial Omani)	0·6529	0·7064	0·7117	0·7006	0·6873
Pakistan (Rupee)	97·6040	107·2052	108·9175	108·417	106·6047
Papua New Guinea (Kina)	5·7436	5·7518	5·7245	5·5303	5·4038
Paraguay (Guarani)	10,556·6188	10,949·034	11,145·829	11,239·12	10,913·66
Peru (New Sol)	7·2490	6·2532	6·2005	5·9931	5·9161
Philippines (Peso)	92·8336	102·9065	103·0777	100·0778	96·8521
Poland (Zloty)	6·2744	6·6646	6·0596	5·5982	5·8289
Portugal (Euro)	1·44	1·474	1·467	1·4626	1·4664
Qatar (Riyal)	6·1714	6·6804	6·7288	6·622	6·4968
Romania (Leu)	56,162·18	59,678·391	58,049·01	1/1/05–30/6/05 53,404·4 1/7/05–31/12/05 5·2643	1/4/05–30/6/05 53,483·7 1/7/05–31/3/06 5·2306
Russia (Rouble–Market)	50·7326	52·6246	52·7342	51·3674	50·4621
Rwanda (R Franc)	922·732	1,026·683	1,031·425	991·2927	967·81
Saudi Arabia (Riyal)	6·3578	6·8814	6·9322	6·8237	6·6944
Seychelles (Rupee)	9·4401	10·1103	10·1938	10·0265	9·8347
Sierra Leone (Leone)	4,046·3759	4,501·4316	4,552·6395	5,017·596	5,130·52
Singapore (S$)	2·9295	3·0974	3·0937	3·0264	2·9663
Solomon Islands (SI$)	12·7742	13·6055	13·6218	13·3353	13·1391
Somali Republic (Schilling)	4,461·972	5,035·7142	5,293·099	4,614·7308	3,841·33
South Africa (Rand)	12·0949	11·81	11·5364	11·5723	11·4532
Spain/Balearic Islands (Euro)	1·44	1·474	1·467	1·4626	1·4664
Sri Lanka (Rupee)	164·0631	185·8561	187·8602	182·1193	180·6214
Sudan (Dinar)	443·2834	472·2258	471·232	442·4396	424·337
Surinam (Guilder)	3,134·437				
(Dollar)		5·0088	5·0407	4·9568	4·8734
Swaziland (Lilangeli)	12·0136	11·7582	11·5018	11·5501	11·4034
Sweden (Krona)	13·1427	13·4526	13·3494	13·5776	13·67855
Switzerland (Franc)	2·2266	2·2757	2·2596	2·2681	2·2756
Syria (Pound)	81·2087	92·1296	94·1199	94·8321	93·0719

Average rates of exchange — continued

Average for year ending	31.3.04	31.12.04	31.3.05	31.12.05	31.3.06
Taiwan (New T$)	57·7063	61·0875	60·6512	58·4213	57·7011
Tanzania (Schilling)	1,797·86	1,995·077	2,008·9023	2,051·1569	2,052·1933
Thailand (Baht)	68·7556	73·7457	73·9875	73·1459	72·1171
Tonga Islands (Pa 'Anga)	2·84	3·6061	3·6002	3·253	3·2585
Trinidad and Tobago (TT$)	10·2507	11·3504	11·488	11·3985	11·1882
Tunisia (Dinar)	2·1393	2·2834	2·3029	2·3573	2·3656
Turkey (Lira)	2,405,776·37	2,614,460·3	1/4/04–31/12/04 2,672,509·6 1/1/05–31/3/05 2·4998	2·4483	2·4068
Uganda (New Shilling)	3,327·7742	3,314·5158	3,248·728	3,234·669	3,221·231
United Arab Emirates (Dirham)	6·2256	6·7388	6·7884	6·6827	6·5562
Uruguay (Peso Uruguayo)	116·9099	52·5696	50·9267	44·461	43·1552
USA (US$)	1·6939	1·8318	1·8445	1·8195	1·79738
Venezuela (Bolivar)	3,629·222	5,128·1466	4,997·8741	4,916·2392	4,751·6019
Vietnam (Dong)	26,564·48	28,839·666	29,110·77	28,797·3333	28,298·4
Yemen (Rial)	306·0884	338·4705	342·6463	348·0178	345·207
Zambia (Kwacha)	8,038·83	8,742·492	8,790·4958	8,104·899	7,310·1153
Zimbabwe (Dollar)	2,499·284	1/1/04–23/1/04 1,505·5 24/01/04–31/12/04 9,319·984		1/1/05–21/10/05 22,764·44 22/10/05–31/12/05 10,335·445	1/4/05–21/10/05 27,676·3 22/10/05–31/3/06
				118,470·7	144,586·5

Rates of exchange on year-end dates

	31.3.04	31.12.04	31.3.05	31.12.05	31.3.06
Australia ($A)	2·4072	2·4491	2·4428	2·3403	2·4326
Austria (Euro)	1·4955	1·4125	1·454	1·4554	1·4333
Belgium (Euro)	1·4955	1·4125	1·454	1·4554	1·4333
Canada (Can$)	2·4154	2·3003	2·2861	2·0054	2·0235
Denmark (Krone)	11·1342	10·5068	10·8316	10·8558	10·6962
European Union (Euro)	1·4955	1·4125	1·454	1·4554	1·4333
France (Euro)	1·4955	1·4125	1·454	1·4554	1·4333
Germany (Euro)	1·4955	1·4125	1·454	1·4554	1·4333
Hong Kong (HK$)	14·3188	14·9229	14·7377	13·3109	13·4598
Irish Republic (Euro)	1·4955	1·4125	1·454	1·4554	1·4333
Italy (Euro)	1·4955	1·4125	1·454	1·4554	1·4333
Japan (Yen)	191·201	196·732	202·112	202·268	204·660
Luxembourg (Euro)	1·4955	1·4125	1·454	1·4554	1·4333
Netherlands (Euro)	1·4955	1·4125	1·454	1·4554	1·4333
Norway (Krone)	12·6185	11·6281	11·9316	11·6245	11·3835
Portugal (Euro)	1·4955	1·4125	1·454	1·4554	1·4333
South Africa (Rand)	11·5831	10·8163	11·7604	10·8885	10·6926
Spain/Balearic Islands (Euro)	1·4955	1·4125	1·454	1·4554	1·4333
Sweden (Krona)	13·8598	12·7584	13·3089	13·6629	13·5185
Switzerland (Franc)	2·3283	2·1832	2·2523	2·2681	2·2668
USA (US$)	1·8378	1·9199	1·8896	1·7168	1·7346

Note: The material on pages 76 to 78 is reproduced from information provided by the HMRC and is Crown copyright.

Double taxation agreements (including protocols and regulations)
Agreements in force covering taxes on income and capital gains

Country	SI/SR & O
Antigua & Barbuda	**1947/2865**
	1968/1096
Argentina	**1997/1777**
Armenia[1]	
Australia	**2003/3199**
Austria	**1970/1947**
	1979/117
	1994/768
Azerbaijan	**1995/762**
Bangladesh	**1980/708**
Barbados	**1970/952**
	1973/2096
Belarus[1]	**1986/224**
Belgium	**1987/2053**
Belize	**1947/2866**
	1968/573
	1973/2097
Bolivia	**1995/2707**
Bosnia Herzegovina[2]	**1981/1815**
Botswana	**1978/183**
Brunei	**1950/1977**
	1968/306
	1973/2098
Bulgaria	**1987/2054**
Canada	**1980/709**
	1980/1528
	1985/1996
	2003/2619
Chile	**2003/3200**
China[4]	**1984/1826**
	1996/3164
Croatia[2]	**1981/1815**
Cyprus	**1975/425**
	1980/1529
Czech Republic[3]	**1991/2876**
Denmark	**1980/1960**
	1991/2877
	1996/3165
Egypt	**1980/1091**
Estonia	**1994/3207**
Falkland Islands	**1997/2985**
Fiji	**1976/1342**
Finland	**1970/153**
	1980/710
	1985/1997
	1991/2878
	1996/3166
France	**1968/1869**
	1973/1328
	1987/466
	1987/2055
Gambia	**1980/1963**
Georgia[1]	**2004/3325**
Germany	**1967/25**
	1971/874
Ghana	**1993/1800**
Greece	**1954/142**
Grenada	**1949/361**
	1968/1867
Guernsey	**1952/1215**
	1994/3209
Guyana	**1992/3207**
Hungary	**1978/1056**

Country	SI/SR & O
Iceland	**1991/2879**
India	**1993/1801**
Indonesia	**1994/769**
Irish Republic	**1976/2151**
	1976/2152
	1995/764
	1998/3151
Isle of Man	**1955/1205**
	1991/2880
	1994/3208
Israel	**1963/616**
	1971/391
Italy	**1990/2590**
Ivory Coast	**1987/169**
Jamaica	1973/1329
Japan	**1970/1948**
	1980/1530
Jersey	**1952/1216**
	1994/3210
Jordan	**2001/3924**
Kazakhstan	**1994/3211**
	1998/2567
Kenya	**1977/1299**
Kiribati (and Tuvalu)	**1950/750**
	1968/309
	1974/1271
Korea (South)	**1996/3168**
Kuwait	**1999/2036**
Kyrgyzstan[1]	
Latvia	**1996/3167**
Lesotho	**1997/2986**
Lithuania[1]	**2001/3925**
	2002/2847
Luxembourg	**1968/1100**
	1980/567
	1984/364
Macedonia[2]	**1981/1815**
Malawi	**1956/619**
	1964/1401
	1968/1101
	1979/302
Malaysia	**1997/2987**
Malta	**1995/763**
Mauritius	**1981/1121**
	1987/467
	2003/2620
Mexico	**1994/3212**
Moldova[1]	
Mongolia	**1996/2598**
Montserrat	**1947/2869**
	1968/576
Morocco	**1991/2881**
Myanmar (Burma)	**1952/751**
Namibia	**1962/2352**
	1967/1490
Netherlands	**1980/1961**
	1990/2152
New Zealand	**1984/365**
	2004/1274
Nigeria	**1987/2057**
Norway	**2000/3247**
Oman	**1998/2568**

Double taxation agreements — continued

Country	SI/SR & O	Country	SI/SR & O
Pakistan	1987/2058	Switzerland	1978/1408
Papua New Guinea	1991/2882		1982/714
Philippines	1978/184		1994/3215
Poland	1978/282		
Portugal	1969/599	Taiwan	2002/3137
		Tajikistan[1]	1986/224
Romania	1977/57	Thailand	1981/1546
Russian Federation	1994/3213	Trinidad and Tobago	1983/1903
		Tunisia	1984/133
St Kitts and Nevis	1947/2872	Turkey	1988/932
Serbia and Montenegro[2]	1981/1815	Turkmenistan[1]	1986/224
Sierra Leone	1947/2873	Tuvalu (and Kirbati)	1950/750
	1968/1104		1968/309
Singapore	1997/2988		1974/1271
Slovak Republic[3]	1991/2876		
Slovenia[2]	1981/1815	Uganda	1993/1802
Solomon Islands	1950/748	Ukraine	1993/1803
	1968/574	USA	2002/2848
	1974/1270	Uzbekistan	1994/770
South Africa	2002/3138		
Spain	1976/1919	Venezuela	1996/2599
	1995/765	Vietnam	1994/3216
Sri Lanka	1980/713		
Sudan	1977/1719	Zambia	1972/1721
Swaziland	1969/380		1981/1816
Sweden	1984/366	Zimbabwe	1982/1842

Notes:

[1] Following the dissolution of the USSR, new agreements have come into force with Azerbaijan, Estonia, Kazakhstan, Latvia, Lithuania, the Russian Federation, Ukraine and Uzbekistan. *SI 1986 No 224* (the former USSR agreement) is treated as continuing to apply to Belarus, Tajikistan and Turkmenistan (in the case of Belarus until the coming into force of *SI 1995 No 2706*). It was similarly so treated by the UK until 31 March 2002 in the case of Armenia, Georgia, Kyrgyzstan, Lithuania and Moldova (none of which considered itself bound by that convention) but as ceasing so to apply after that date (although new treaties are in force with Lithuania and Georgia). (SP 4/01).

[2] *SI 1981 No 1815* (the former Yugoslavia agreement) is treated as remaining in force between the UK and, respectively, Bosnia-Herzegovina, Croatia, Macedonia, Serbia and Montenegro and Slovenia. (SP 3/2004). Negotiations for a new double taxation convention are taking place with Croatia, Serbia and Montenegro and Slovenia and negotiations are planned with Macedonia. (Revenue Press Release, 29 September 2004).

[3] *SI 1991 No 2876* (the former Czechoslovakia agreement) is treated as remaining in force between the UK and, respectively, the Czech Republic and the Slovak Republic. (SP 5/93).

[4] *SI 1984 No 1826* does not apply to the Hong Kong Special Administrative Region.

Agreements in force covering shipping and air transport profits

Country	SI or SR & O	Country	SI or SR & O
Algeria (air)	1984/362	Iran (air)	1960/2419
Armenia (USSR air)*	1974/1269	Jordan	1979/300
Belarus (USSR air)*	1974/1269	Kyrgyzstan (USSR air)*	1974/1269
Brazil	1968/572	Lebanon	1964/278
Cameroon (air)	1982/1841	Moldova (USSR air)*	1974/1269
China (air)	1981/1119	Saudi Arabia (air)	1994/767
Congo Democratic Republic	1977/1298	Tajikistan (USSR air)*	1974/1269
Ethiopia (air)	1977/1297	Turkmenistan (USSR air)*	1974/1269
Georgia (USSR air)*	1974/1269		
Hong Kong (air)	1998/2566		
(shipping)	2000/3248		

* HMRC have confirmed that this Arrangement will be treated in the same way as the Convention covering income and capital gains (SI 1986/224). See note 1 on p 80.

Agreements in force covering estates, inheritances and gifts

France*	1963/1319	Pakistan*	1957/1522
India*	1956/998	South Africa	1979/576
Ireland	1978/1107	Sweden	1981/840
Italy*	1968/304		1989/986
Netherlands	1980/706	Switzerland	1994/3214
	1996/730	USA	1979/1454

* Agreements pre-date UK inheritance tax/capital transfer tax.

Overseas income – basis of assessment

	Professions, trades, etc	Pensions	Other income
NON-RESIDENTS	Exempt	Exempt	Exempt
RESIDENTS 1) **Foreign domicile**	Remittance	Remittance	Remittance
2) **UK domicile** (a) Non Commonwealth citizen[1]	Arising	90%[3] arising	Arising
(b) Commonwealth citizen[2] (i) ordinarily resident	Arising	90%[3] arising	Arising
(ii) not ordinarily resident	Remittance	Remittance	Remittance

[1] But not citizen of the Republic of Ireland.
[2] Or citizen of the Republic of Ireland.
[3] Pensions paid by the governments of the Federal Republic of Germany or of Austria to victims of Nazi persecution are exempt.

It was announced in the Budget Speech on 17 April 2002 that the Government is reviewing the residence and domicile rules as they affect the tax liabilities of individuals (2002) SWTI 521.

Employment income liability of non-resident employees   see p 56.

Tax-free (FOTRA) securities

Interest on all government stock is exempt from tax where the beneficial owner is not ordinarily resident in the UK (FA 1996 s 154; FA 1998 s 161; ITTOIA 2005 ss 713, 714). Except in the case of 3½% War Loan 1952 or after, the exemption does not apply where the securities are held for the purposes of a trade or business carried on in the UK.

Social security benefits

Taxable state benefits

	Weekly 10.4.06 onwards £	Total 2006–07 (52 weeks) £	Weekly 11.4.05 onwards £	Total 2005–06 (52 weeks) £
Bereavement benefits[1]				
Standard rate (widow's pension)	84.25	4,381	82.05	4,266
Widowed parent's allowance	84.25	4,381	82.05	4,266
Carer's allowance	46.95	2,441	45.70	2,376
–Adult dependency increase	28.05	1,458	27.30	1,419
Incapacity benefit				
Long-term (after 52 weeks)	78.50	4,082	76.45	3,975
–Adult dependency increase	46.95	2,441	45.70	2,376
–Age increase: higher rate	16.50	858	16.05	834
lower rate	8.25	429	8.05	418
Short term[2]				
–Under pension age: higher rate	70.05	–	68.20	–
–Adult dependency increase	36.60	–	35.65	–
–Over pension age: higher rate	78.50	–	76.45	–
–Adult dependency increase	45.15	–	43.95	–
Industrial death benefit[3]				
Widow's pension higher rate	84.25	4,381	82.05	4,266
lower rate	25.28	1,314	24.62	1,280
Widower's pension	84.25	4,381	82.05	4,266
Invalidity allowance[4]				
Higher rate	16.50	858	16.05	834
Middle rate	10.60	551	10.30	535
Lower rate	5.30	275	5.15	267
Jobseeker's allowance[5]				
Single: under 18	34.60	–	33.85	–
18 to 24	45.50	–	44.50	–
25 or over	57.45	–	56.20	–
State pension				
Single person (Category A or B)	84.25	4,381	82.05	4,266
Couple –if both contributors	168.50	8,762	164.10	8,533
–if wife non-contributor	134.75	7,007	131.20	6,822
Adult dependency increase	50.50	2,626	49.15	2,555
Non-contributory pension				
–single (Category C or D)	50.50	2,626	49.15	2,555
–couple (Category C)	80.70	4,196	78.55	4,084
–couple (Category D–over 80)	101.00	5,252	98.30	5,111
Age addition (over 80) (each)	0.25	13	0.25	13
Statutory adoption pay				
Rate[6]	108.85	–	106.00	–
Earnings threshold	84.00	–	82.00	–
Statutory maternity pay				
Rate[6]	108.85	–	106.00	–
Earnings threshold	84.00	–	82.00	–
Statutory paternity pay				
Rate[6]	108.85	–	106.00	–
Earnings threshold	84.00	–	82.00	–
Statutory sick pay				
Rate	70.05	–	68.20	–
Earnings threshold	84.00	–	82.00	–

[1] Paid to widows and widowers for up to 52 weeks.
[2] For weeks 29 to 52. See note below on non-taxable benefits on page 83.
[3] For deaths before 11 April 1988 only.
[4] When paid with retirement pensions. See note below on non-taxable benefits on page 83.
[5] Where the allowance exceeds the amount shown above, the excess is not taxable.
[6] The allowance is 90% of average weekly earnings if less than the above amount. In the first six weeks the rate of SMP is 90% of average weekly earnings even if higher than the standard rate.

Non-taxable state benefits

Weekly rates from		9/4/07	10.04.06	11.04.05
			£	£
Attendance allowance				
Higher rate (day and night)			62.25	60.60
Lower rate (day or night)		43.15	41.65	40.55
Child benefit				
Eldest child (couple)			17.45	17.00
Eldest child (lone parent)			17.55	17.55
Each subsequent child			11.70	11.40
Child dependency addition				
Paid with retirement pension, bereavement benefit, carer's allowance, incapacity benefit, higher rate industrial death benefit			11.35	11.35
Disability living allowance				
Care component	higher rate		62.25	60.60
	middle rate		41.65	40.55
	lower rate		16.50	16.05
Mobility component	higher rate		43.45	42.30
	lower rate		16.50	16.05
Guardian's allowance			12.50	12.20
Incapacity benefit (short-term)*				
Under pension age — lower rate (first 28 weeks)			59.20	57.65
—Adult dependency increase			36.60	35.65
Over pension age — lower rate (first 28 weeks)			75.35	73.35
—Adult dependency increase			45.15	43.95
Maternity allowance (where SMP not available)				
Standard rate			108.85	106.00
MA threshold			30.00	30.00
—Adult dependency increase			36.60	35.65
Severe disablement allowance				
Basic rate			47.45	46.20
Age-related additon	higher rate		16.50	16.05
	middle rate		10.60	10.30
	lower rate		5.30	5.15
—Adult dependency increase			28.25	27.50

* Incapacity benefit replaced invalidity allowance from April 1995. The benefits are taxable except those paid in the first 28 weeks of incapacity and those paid to persons already receiving invalidity benefit on 13 April 1995 so long as they remain incapable of work.

Other non-taxable benefits include:

Bereavement payment (lump sum £2,000)
Child tax credit (see Tax Credits – p 67)
Christmas bonus (with retirement pension)
Cold weather payments
Council tax benefit (income related)
Earnings top-up
Housing benefit (income related)
Income support (income related)
Industrial death benefit
Industrial injuries disablement pension
Jobfinder's grant
Pension credit (see Tax Credits, p 67)
Pneumoconiosis, byssinosis and miscellaneous disease benefits
Redundancy payment
Social fund payments
Television licence payment
Vaccine damage (lump sum)
War pensions
Winter fuel payment (£200 plus £100 for those aged over 80)
Working tax credit (see Tax Credits, p 67)

Stamp taxes

Stamp duty land tax

Stamp duty land tax applies to contracts entered into (or varied) after 10 July 2003 and completed after 30 November 2003 and to leases granted after that date. With effect from 22 July 2004, it also applies to the transfer of an interest in land into, or out of, a partnership and to the acquisition of an interest in a partnership where the partnership property includes an interest in land. With effect from 19 July 2006, it applies to transfers of partnership interests only where the sole or main activity of the partnership is investing or dealing in interests in land.

Land transactions	Consideration[1]		
Effective date	Residential property	Non-residential or mixed property	Rate
From 23.3.06	Up to £125,000	Up to £150,000	Nil
	£125,001–£250,000	£150,001–£250,000	1%
	£250,001–£500,000	£250,001–£500,000	3%
	£500,001 or more	£500,001 or more	4%
17.3.05–22.3.06	Up to £120,000	Up to £150,000	Nil
	£120,001–£250,000	£150,001–£250,000	1%
	£250,001–£500,000	£250,001–£500,000	3%
	£500,001 or more	£500,001 or more	4%
1.12.03–16.3.05	Up to £60,000	Up to £150,000	Nil
	£60,001–£250,000	£150,001–£250,000	1%
	£250,001–£500,000	£250,001–£500,000	3%
	£500,001 or more	£500,001 or more	4%
Lease rentals	On net present value of rent over term of lease (applying a discount rate of 3.5%)[2]		
Effective date	Residential property	Non-residential or mixed property	Rate
From 23.3.06	Up to £125,000	Up to £150,000	Nil
	£125,001 or more	£150,001 or more	1%
17.3.05–22.3.06	Up to £120,000	Up to £150,000	Nil
	£120,001 or more	£150,001 or more	1%
1.12.03–16.3.05	Up to £60,000	Up to £150,000	Nil
	£60,001or more	£150,001 or more	1%

Premiums
The same tax is payable for a premium granted as for a land transaction (except that special rules apply to a premium where the rent exceeds £600 a year).

[1] Rates apply to the full consideration, not only to that in excess of the previous band.
[2] Rates apply to the amount of npv in the slice, not the whole value.

Exemptions and reliefs

No SDLT (or stamp duty) is chargeable on:

(1) transfers to charities for use for charitable purposes
(2) transfers to bodies established for national purposes
(3) gifts inter vivos
(4) land transfers within groups of companies
(5) land transferred in exchange for shares on company reconstruction and acquisitions
(6) transfers of intellectual property
(7) certain transfers to registered social landlords
(8) certain leases granted by registered social landlords
(9) transfers of goodwill (after 21.4.02)
(10) sale and leaseback arrangements involving commercial property (after 30.11.03) (extended with effect from 22.7.04 to residential property and lease and leaseback transactions)
(11) certain acquisitions of residential property by house building companies or property traders when people move into a new dwelling or a chain of transactions break down, or by employers involving employee relocations (after 31.11.03) (extended with effect from 22.7.04 for people buying a new home and unable to move into it immediately)
(12) (after 30.11.03 and before 22.3.06) initial acquisition of assets by trustees of a unit trust scheme
(13) transfers of property to beneficiaries under a will or an intestacy (after 30.11.03)
(14) certain transfers on divorce
(15) transfers on sale of residential property for a consideration of up to £150,000 in disadvantaged parts of the UK. This also applies to leases broadly, where the relevant rental value does not exceed £150,000 and to premiums unless the annual rent exceeds £600. From 10 April 2003 to 16 March 2005, the exemption also applied to transfers and leases of non-residential properties of any value. (Before 10 April 2003, it applied to transfers and leases for both residential and non-residential properties up to £150,000.) See SI 2001/3747 for areas designated as disadvantaged.

Stamp duty

For contracts entered into (or varied) after 10 July 2003 and completed after 30 November 2003 and for leases granted after that date, stamp duty is abolished for all transfers other than stocks and marketable securities, and interests in partnerships. From 22 July 2004 stamp duty is also abolished for certain partnership transactions involving an interest in land. From those dates, transfers of land are subject to stamp duty land tax (see p 84).

Transfers of stock and marketable securities		0·5%
Other transfers (including land transactions before the introduction of SDLT)		
	16.3.99–27.3.00	28.3.00–30.11.03
On transfer made pursuant to contract after	9.3.99	21.3.00
Conveyance or transfer on sale with certificate of value[1]		
Not exceeding £60,000	Nil	Nil
£60,001–£250,000	1%	1%
£250,001–£500,000	2·5%	3%
£500,001 or more	3·5%	4%
Conveyance or transfer on sale without certificate of value	3·5%	4%
Lease premiums The same duty is payable for a premium granted as for a conveyance or transfer on sale (except that special rules apply to a premium where the rent exceeds £600 a year).		
Lease rentals (before the introduction of SDLT) Furnished residential accommodation for definite term of less than 1 year at rent in excess of £5,000	£5	
Leases not exceeding 7 years, or for an indefinite term:		
—Up to £5,000 (£500 before 28.3.00) p.a.	Nil	
—Over £5,000 (£500 before 28.3.00) p.a.	1%	
Leases over 7 years and up to 35 years	2%	
Leases over 35 years and up to 100 years	12%	
Leases over 100 years	24%	

[1] These rates apply to the full consideration, not only to that in excess of the previous band.

Rounding
Stamp duty is rounded up to the next multiple of £5 in all cases other than for SDRT.

Fixed duties (before the introduction of SDLT)
Leases other than above	£5
Declaration of trust; duplicate or counterpart; exchange or partition; release or renunciation; surrender	£5

Stamp Duty Reserve Tax (SDRT)

Agreements to transfer chargeable securities for money or money's worth (eg renounceable letters of allotment)[1]	0.5%
Chargeable securities put into a clearance service[2] or converted into depositary receipts	1.5%
Dealings of units in unit trusts and shares in open-ended investment companies[3]	0.5%
Transfers of foreign currency bearer shares and agreements to transfer sterling or foreign currency convertible or equity-related loan stock issued by UK companies	0.5%

[1] If the transaction is completed by a duly stamped instrument within 6 years from the date on which the charge is imposed, the SDRT will be cancelled or repaid.
[2] Where the operator of a clearance service elects to collect and account for SDRT on the normal rate of 0.5% on dealing within the system the higher SDRT charge of 1.5% does not apply.
[3] From 6 April 2001 transfers of units in a unit trust and surrenders of shares in open-ended investment trusts are exempt when held within individual pension accounts.

Stamp taxes — continued

Interest on unpaid tax

Stamp duty land tax. *From 26 September 2005*: Interest runs from the end of 30 days after the effective date of transaction (normally completion), or the date of a disqualifying event, until the tax is paid. In the case of a deferred payment, interest runs from the date the payment is due until the tax is paid. A penalty carries interest from the date determined until the date of payment.

Stamp duty. *For instruments executed from 1 October 1999*: Interest runs from the end of 30 days after the date the instrument is executed until the tax is paid. Amounts less than £25 are not charged.

Stamp duty reserve tax. Interest is charged from 14 days after the transaction date for exchange transactions and otherwise from seven days after the end of the month of the transaction. Amounts less than £25 are not charged.

Rates: see p 5.

Repayment supplement

Stamp duty land tax. *From 26 September 2005*: Interest is added to repayments of overpaid stamp duty land tax and runs from the date tax was paid or an amount was lodged with HMRC, or the date a penalty was made, to the date the order for repayment is issued.

Stamp duty. *For instruments executed from 1 October 1999*: Interest is added to repayments of overpaid stamp duty and runs from 30 days after the date the instrument is executed or the date of payment if later. Amounts less than £25 are not paid.

Stamp duty reserve tax. Interest is paid from 14 days after the transaction date for exchange transactions and otherwise from seven days after the end of the month of the transaction.

Rates: see p 8.

Penalties

Offence	*Penalty*
Stamp duty – for instruments executed from 1 October 1999	
Failure to present instrument for stamping within 30 days after execution (or the day in which it is first received in the UK if executed outside the UK) (Stamp Act 1891 s 15B; SI 1999/2537). (Extended to instruments executed from 24 July 2002 for transfers of UK land and buildings, wherever executed (FA 2002 s 114)).	If presented within one year after the end of the 30 day period: the lower of £300 or the amount of the unpaid duty. If presented more than one year after the end of the 30 day period: the greater of £300 or the amount of unpaid duty.
Stamp duty land tax – contracts completed after 30 November 2003	
Failure to deliver a land transaction return by the filing date (FA 2003 Sch 10 paras 3, 4).	£100 if return delivered within 3 months of filing date, otherwise £200. If not delivered within 12 months, penalty up to amount of tax chargeable.
Failure to comply with notice to deliver return within specified period (FA 2003 Sch 10 para 5).	Up to £60 for each day on which the failure continues after notification.
Fraudulently or negligently delivering an incorrect return or failing to remedy an error without unreasonable delay (FA 2003 Sch 10 para 8).	Up to the difference between the amount payable and the amount that would have been chargeable on the basis of the return delivered.
Fraudulently or negligently giving a self-certificate for a chargeable transaction or failing to remedy an error in respect of such certificate without unreasonable delay (FA 2003 Sch 11 para 3).	Up to the amount of tax chargeable.
Failure to keep and preserve records under FA 2003 Sch 10 para 9 or Sch 11 para 4 (FA 2003 Sch 10 para 11, Sch 11 para 6).	Up to £3,000 unless the information is provided by other documentary evidence.
Failure to comply with notice to produce documents etc under FA 2003 Sch 10 para 14 or Sch 11 para 9 (FA 2003 Sch 10 para 16, Sch 11 para 11).	(a) Initial penalty of £50; (b) further penalty for each day the failure continues up to £30 if penalty determined by HMRC, or £150 if determined by the court.
Failure (from 1 August 2005) to disclose certain SDLT proposals or arrangements (SI 2005/1868; SI 2005/1869).	(a) Initial penalty up to £5,000; (b) further penalty up to £600 per day while failure continues.

Value added tax

Rates

	Rate	VAT fraction
Standard rate	17.5%	7/47
Reduced rate (see page 90)	5%	1/21
Flat-rate scheme for farmers	4%*	

* Flat rate addition to sale price

Registration limits

UK taxable supplies
A person who makes taxable supplies is liable to be registered:
(a) at the end of any month, or
(b) at any time, if:

	(a) turnover in the past year[1] (b) turnover in the next 30 days[2] exceeds:	Unless, in the case of (a), turnover for next year not expected to exceed:
1.4.06 onwards	£61,000	£59,000
1.4.05–31.3.06	£60,000	£58,000
1.4.04–31.3.05	£58,000	£56,000
10.4.03–31.3.04	£56,000	£54,000
25.4.02–9.4.03	£55,000	£53,000
1.4.01–24.4.02	£54,000	£52,000
1.4.00–31.3.01	£52,000	£50,000

[1] The value of taxable supplies in the year then ending.
[2] If there are reasonable grounds for believing the value of taxable supplies will exceed limit.

Supplies from other EC countries ('distance selling')
A business person in another EC country not registered or liable to be registered in the UK is liable to be registered on any day if, in the period beginning with 1 January in that year, the value of supplies by that person to non-taxable persons in the UK exceeds:

1.1.93 onwards	£70,000

Acquisitions from other EC countries
A person not registered or liable to be registered under the above rules is liable to be registered
(a) at the end of any month if, in the period beginning with 1 January in that year, the value of taxable goods acquired by that person for business purposes (or for non-business purposes if a public body, charity, club, etc) from suppliers in other EC countries exceeds the following limits; or
(b) at any time, if there are reasonable grounds for believing the value of such acquisitions in the next 30 days will exceed the following limits:

1.4.06 onwards	£61,000
1.4.05–31.3.06	£60,000
1.4.04–31.3.05	£58,000
10.4.03–31.3.04	£56,000
25.4.02–9.4.03	£55,000
1.4.01–24.4.02	£54,000
1.4.00–31.3.01	£52,000

Value added tax — continued

Deregistration limits

UK taxable supplies

A registered taxable person ceases to be liable to be registered if, at any time, HMRC are satisfied that the value of taxable supplies in the year then beginning will not exceed:

1.4.06 onwards	£59,000
1.4.05–31.3.06	£58,000
1.4.04–31.3.05	£56,000
10.4.03–31.3.04	£54,000
25.4.02–9.4.03	£53,000
1.4.01–24.4.02	£52,000
1.4.00–31.3.01	£50,000

Unless the reason for not exceeding the limit during that year is that the person will cease making taxable supplies or suspend making taxable supplies for 30 days or more.

Supplies from other EC countries ('distance selling')

A person registered under these provisions ceases to be liable to be registered if, at any time
(a) relevant supplies in the year ended 31 December last before that time did not exceed the following limit; and
(b) HMRC are satisfied that the value of relevant supplies in the year immediately following that year will not exceed the following limit:

1.1.93 onwards	£70,000

Acquisitions from other EC countries

A person registered under these provisions ceases to be liable to be registered if, at any time
(a) relevant acquisitions in the year ended 31 December last before that time did not exceed the following limits; and
(b) HMRC are satisfied that the value of relevant acquisitions in the year immediately following that year will not exceed the following limits:

1.4.06 onwards	£61,000
1.4.05–31.3.06	£60,000
1.4.04–31.3.05	£58,000
10.4.03–31.3.04	£56,000
25.4.02–9.4.03	£55,000
1.4.01–24.4.02	£54,000
1.4.00–31.3.01	£52,000

Annual accounting scheme

A business may, subject to conditions, complete one VAT return a year. Before 1 April 2006, only businesses with taxable turnover up to £150,000 could join the scheme immediately; other businesses had to have been registered for 12 months.

	Can join if taxable supplies in next year not expected to exceed:	Must leave at end of accounting year if taxable supplies exceeded:
1.4.06 onwards	£1,350,000	£1,600,000
1.4.04–31.3.06	£660,000	£825,000
1.4.01–31.3.04	£600,000	£750,000

Cash accounting scheme

A business may, subject to conditions, account for and pay VAT on the basis of cash paid and received. It can join the scheme at any time as follows.

	Can join if taxable supplies in next year not expected to exceed:	Must leave at end of accounting year if taxable supplies exceed:	Unless turnover for next year not expected to exceed:
1.4.04 onwards	£660,000	£825,000	£660,000
1.4.01–31.3.04	£600,000	£750,000	£600,000
Before 31.3.01	£350,000	£437,500	£350,000

Flat-rate scheme for small businesses

A business which expects its taxable supplies (excluding VAT) in the next year to be no more than £150,000 and its total business income to be no more than £187,500 can opt to join a flat-rate scheme. The appropriate percentage below is applied to total turnover generated, including exempt income, to calculate net VAT due.

Category of business	*Appropriate %*	
	before 1.1.04	**from 1.1.04**
Accountancy or book-keeping	13·5	13
Advertising	11	9·5
Agricultural services	9	7·5
Animal husbandry	11	N/A
Any other activity not listed elsewhere	11	10
Architect	13·5	12·5
Boarding or care of animals	N/A	10·5
Business services that are not listed elsewhere	12·5	11
Catering services, including restaurants and takeaways	13	12
Civil and structural engineer or surveyor	N/A	12·5
Computer and IT consultancy or data processing	14·5	13
Computer repair services	13·5	11
Dealing in waste or scrap	11	9·5
Entertainment or journalism	12	11
Estate agency and property management services	11·5	11
Farming or agriculture that is not listed elsewhere	6·5	6
Film, radio, television or video production	N/A	10·5
Financial services	12	11·5
Forestry or fishing	10	9
General building or construction services[1]	9	8·5
Hairdressing or other beauty treatment services	13	12
Hiring or renting goods	9·5	8·5
Hotel or accommodation	10·5	9·5
Investigation or security	11	10
Labour-only building or construction services[1]	14·5	13·5
Laundry or dry-cleaning services	12	11
Lawyer or legal services	13·5	13
Library, archive, museum or other cultural activity	8·5	7·5
Management consultancy	13·5	12·5
Manufacturing fabricated metal products	11	10
Manufacturing food	8·5	7·5
Manufacturing that is not listed elsewhere	10	8·5
Manufacturing yarn, textiles or clothing	9·5	8·5
Membership organisation	7	5·5
Mining or quarrying	10	9
Packaging	9	8·5
Photography	10	9·5
Post offices[2] (from 1 April 2004)	N/A	2
Postal and courier services[3] (before 1 April 2004)	6	5·5
Printing	8·5	7·5
Publishing	10	9·5
Pubs	6	5·5
Real estate activity not listed elsewhere	13	12
Repairing personal or household goods	10	8·5
Repairing vehicles	8·5	7·5
Retailing food, confectionery, tobacco, newspapers or children's clothing	5	2
Retailing pharmaceuticals, medical goods, cosmetics or toiletries	8	7
Retailing that is not listed elsewhere	7	6
Retailing vehicles or fuel	8	7
Secretarial services	11·5	11
Social work	9	8·5
Sport or recreation	8	7
Transport or storage, couriers, freight, removals and taxis[3]	10	9
Travel agency	10	9
Veterinary medicine	11	9·5
Wholesaling agricultural products	7	6
Wholesaling food	7	5·5
Wholesaling that is not listed elsewhere	8	7

[1] 'Labour-only building or construction services' means services where the value of materials supplied is less than 10% of turnover of such services; any other services are 'general building or construction services'.
[2] From 1 April 2004 a rate of 2% applies to Post Offices. Previously they fell within the category for postal and courier services.
[3] From 1 April 2004 (1 July 2004 for courier businesses that applied to join the scheme before 3 March 2004) couriers must apply the rate for transport).

Value added tax — continued

Partial exemption

A registered person who makes taxable and exempt supplies is partly exempt and may not be able to deduct (or reclaim) all his input tax. Where, however, input tax attributable to exempt supplies in a prescribed accounting period or tax year is within the de minimis limits below, all such input tax is attributable to taxable supplies and recoverable (subject to the normal rules).

De minimis limits	£625 per month on average and 50% of all input tax for the period concerned

Capital goods scheme

Input tax adjustment following change in taxable use of capital goods

Item	Value	Adjustment period
Computer equipment	£50,000 or more	5 years
Land and buildings	£250,000 or more	10 years (5 years where interest had less than 10 years to run on acquisition)

Adjustment formula

$$\frac{\text{Total input tax on item}}{\text{Length of adjustment period}} \times \text{adjustment percentage}$$

The adjustment percentage is the percentage change in the extent to which the item is used (or treated as used) in making taxable supplies between the first interval in the adjustment period and a subsequent interval. (The first interval generally ends on the last day of the tax year in which the input tax was incurred.)

Zero-rated supplies

A zero-rated supply is a taxable supply, but the rate of tax is nil.
(VATA 1994 Sch 8)
Group 1—Food
Group 2—Sewerage services and water
Group 3—Books etc
Group 4—Talking books for the blind and handicapped and wireless sets for the blind
Group 5—Construction of buildings etc
Group 6—Protected buildings
Group 7—International services
Group 8—Transport
Group 9—Caravans and houseboats
Group 10—Gold
Group 11—Bank notes
Group 12—Drugs, medicines, aids for the handicapped etc
Group 13—Imports, exports etc
Group 15—Charities etc
Group 16—Clothing and footwear

Reduced rate supplies

(VATA 1994 Sch 7A)
Group 1—Domestic fuel and power
Group 2—Installation of energy-saving materials
Group 3—Grant-funded installation of heating equipment or security goods or connection of a gas supply
Group 4—Women's sanitary products
Group 5—Children's car seats
Group 6—Residential conversions
Group 7—Residential renovations and alterations
Group 8—Contraceptive products (from 1 July 2006)
Group 9—Welfare advice or information (from 1 July 2006)

Exempt supplies

(VATA 1994 Sch 9)
Group 1—Land
Group 2—Insurance
Group 3—Postal services
Group 4—Betting, gaming and lotteries
Group 5—Finance
Group 6—Education
Group 7—Health and welfare
Group 8—Burial and cremation
Group 9—Subscriptions to trade unions, professional and other public interest bodies
Group 10—Sport, sports competitions and physical education
Group 11—Works of art etc
Group 12—Fund-raising events by charities and other qualifying bodies
Group 13—Cultural services etc
Group 14—Supplies of goods where input tax cannot be recovered
Group 15—Investment gold

Car fuel

VAT-inclusive scale figures are used to assess VAT due on petrol provided at below cost price for private journeys by registered traders or their employees, where the petrol has been provided from business resources. The figures represent the tax-inclusive value of the fuel supplied to each individual and relate to return periods beginning on the dates shown.

	12 months £	VAT due per car £	3 months £	VAT due per car £	1 month £	VAT due per car £
From 1 May 2006						
Diesel engine						
2,000cc or less	1,040	154·89	260	38·72	86	12·81
Over 2,000cc	1,325	197·34	331	49·30	110	16·38
Any other type of engine						
1,400cc or less	1,095	163·09	273	40·66	91	13·55
Over 1,400cc up to 2,000cc	1,385	206·28	346	51·53	115	17·13
Over 2,000cc	2,035	303·09	508	75·66	169	25·17
1 May 2005–30 April 2006						
Diesel engine						
2,000cc or less	945	140·74	236	35·15	78	11·62
Over 2,000cc	1,200	178·72	300	44·68	100	14·89
Any other type of engine						
1,400cc or less	985	146·70	246	36·64	82	12·21
Over 1,400cc up to 2,000cc	1,245	185·43	311	46·32	103	15·34
Over 2,000cc	1,830	272·55	457	68·06	152	22·64
1 May 2004–30 April 2005						
Diesel engine						
2,000cc or less	865	128·82	216	32·17	72	10·72
Over 2,000cc	1,095	163·08	273	40·65	91	13·55
Any other type of engine						
1,400cc or less	930	138·51	232	34·55	77	11·46
Over 1,400cc up to 2,000cc	1,175	175·00	293	43·63	97	14·44
Over 2,000cc	1,730	257·65	432	64·34	144	21·44
1 May 2003–30 April 2004						
Diesel engine						
2,000cc or less	900	134·04	225	33·51	75	11·17
Over 2,000cc	1,135	169·04	283	42·14	94	14·00
Any other type of engine						
1,400cc or less	950	141·48	237	35·29	79	11·76
Over 1,400cc up to 2,000cc	1,200	178·72	300	44·68	100	14·89
Over 2,000cc	1,770	263·61	442	65·82	147	21·89
1 May 2002–30 April 2003						
Diesel engine						
2,000cc or less	850	126·59	212	31·57	70	10·42
Over 2,000cc	1,075	160·10	268	39·91	89	13·25
Any other type of engine						
1,400cc or less	905	134·78	226	33·65	75	11·17
Over 1,400cc up to 2,000cc	1,145	170·53	286	42·59	95	14·14
Over 2,000cc	1,690	251·70	422	62·85	140	20·85
6 April 2001–30 April 2002						
Diesel engine						
2,000cc or less	900	134.04	225	33.51	75	11.17
Over 2,000cc	1,145	170.53	286	42.59	95	14.14
Any other type of engine						
1,400cc or less	970	144.46	242	36.04	80	11.91
Over 1,400cc up to 2,000cc	1,230	183.19	307	45.72	102	15.19
Over 2,000cc	1,815	270.31	453	67.46	151	22.48

Value added tax — continued

Interest and penalties

Default interest
(VATA 1999 s 74)
Interest runs on the amount of any VAT assessed (or paid late by voluntary disclosure)
- from the reckonable date (normally the latest date on which a return is required for the period in question)
- until the date of payment (although in practice it runs to the date shown on the notice of assessment or notice of voluntary disclosure if paid within 30 days of that date).

The period of interest cannot commence more than three years before the date of assessment or payment.
The rates of interest are as follows:

Period	Rate
From 6 September 2005	6.5%
6 September 2004–5 September 2005	7.5%
6 December 2003–5 September 2004	6.5%
6 August 2003–5 December 2003	5.5%*
6 November 2001–5 August 2003	6.5%
6 May 2001–5 November 2001	7.5%
6 February 2000–5 May 2001	8.5%
6 March 1999–5 February 2000	7.5%

Interest on VAT overpaid in cases of official error
(VATA 1994 s 78)
Where VAT has been overpaid or underclaimed due to an error by HMRC, then on a claim HMRC must pay interest
- from the date they receive payment (or authorise a repayment) for the return period in question
- until the date on which they authorise payment of the amount on which interest is due.

This provision does not require HMRC to pay interest on an amount on which repayment supplement is due.
The rates of interest are as follows:

Period	Rate
From 6 September 2005	3%
6 September 2004–5 September 2005	4%
6 December 2003–5 September 2004	3%
6 August 2003–5 December 2003	2%*
6 November 2001–5 August 2003	3%
6 May 2001–5 November 2001	4%
6 February 2000–5 May 2001	5%
6 March 1999–5 February 2000	4%

* Due to an administrative error the rate of default and statutory interest was too high by one percentage point between 6 August 2003 and 5 September 2003. HMRC will not seek to recover amounts overpaid by HMRC and will seek to identify businesses overcharged (see Business Brief 17/05 as of 9 September 2005).

Repayment supplement VAT
(VATA 1994 s 79)
Where a person is entitled to a repayment of VAT, the payment due is increased by a supplement of the greater of
(i) 5% of that amount; or
(ii) £50.

The supplement will only be paid if
(a) the return or claim is received by HMRC not later than the last day on which it is required to be made;
(b) HMRC do not issue a written instruction making the refund within the relevant period; and
(c) the amount shown on the return or claim does not exceed the amount due by more than 5% of that amount or £250 whichever is the greater.

The 'relevant period' is 30 days beginning with the receipt of the return or claim or, if later, the day after the last day of the VAT period to which the return or claim relates.

Penalties and surcharges

Offence	Penalty
Failure to submit return or pay VAT due within time limit (where a return is late but the VAT is paid on time or no VAT is due, a default is recorded but no surcharge arises) (VATA 1994 s 59). Failure to pay tax due under the payment on account scheme on time (VATA 1994 s 59A).	The greater of £30 and a specified percentage of outstanding VAT for period, depending on number of defaults in surcharge period: 1st default in period 2%, 2nd default 5%, 3rd default 10%, 4th and further defaults 15%. (Surcharge assessments are not issued for sums of less than £200 unless the rate of the surcharge is 10% or more.)
Evasion of VAT: conduct involving dishonesty (VATA 1994 s 60).	Amount of tax evaded or sought to be evaded (subject to mitigation).
Issuing incorrect certificate stating that certain supplies fall to be zero-rated or taxed at the reduced rate (VATA 1994 s 62).	Difference between tax actually charged and tax which should have been charged.
Misdeclaration or neglect (VATA 1994 s 63).	15% of VAT which would have been lost if inaccuracy had not been discovered.
Repeated misdeclarations (VATA 1994 s 64).	15% of VAT which would have been lost if second and subsequent inaccuracies within penalty period had not been discovered.
Material inaccuracy in EC sales statement (VATA 1994 s 65).	£100 for each material inaccuracy in 2-year penalty period (which commences following notice of second material inaccuracy).
Failure to submit an EC sales statement (VATA 1994 s 66).	Greater of £50 or a daily penalty (maximum 100 days) £5 for the 1st, £10 for the 2nd, £15 for the 3rd or subsequent failure in the default period.
Failure to notify liability for registration or a change in nature of supplies by person exempted from registration (VATA 1994 s 67).	Greater of £50 and a specified percentage of the tax for which the person would have been liable, depending on the period of failure: 9 months or less 5%; over 9 and up to 18 months 10%; over 18 months 15%.
Failure to notify acquisition of excise duty goods or new means of transport (VATA 1994 s 67).	Greater of £50 and: 5% of the tax for which the person would have been liable if period of failure is 3 months or less, 10% if over 3 and up to 6 months and 15% if over 6 months.
Unauthorised issue of invoices (VATA 1994 s 67).	Greater of £50 and 15% of amount shown as or representing VAT.
Breach of walking possession agreement (VATA 1994 s 68).	50% of VAT due or amount recoverable.
Failure to preserve records for prescribed period. Failure to preserve records specified in HMRC direction (VATA 1994 ss 69, 69B).	£500. £200 for each day of failure (maximum 30 days).
Breaches of regulatory provisions, including failure to notify cessation of liability or entitlement to be registered, failure to keep records and non-compliance with any regulations made under VATA 1994 (VATA 1994 s 69). Where failure consists of not paying VAT or not making a return in the required time.	Greater of £50 and a daily penalty (maximum 100 days) of a specified amount depending on number of failures in preceding two years: £5* per day if no previous failures; £10* per day if 1 previous failure; £15* per day if 2 or more previous failures. *1/6th, 1/3rd and 1/2 of 1% of the VAT due respectively, if greater.
Breaches of regulatory provisions involving failure to pay VAT or submit return by due date (VATA 1994 s 69).	Greater of £50 and a daily penalty (for no more than 100 days) of a specified amount depending on number of failures in preceding two years: greater of £5 and ⅙% of VAT due if no previous failures; greater of £10 and ⅓% of VAT due if 1 previous failure; greater of £15 and ½% of VAT due if 2 or more previous failures.
Failure to comply with VAT tribunal directions or summons (VATA 1994 Sch 12 para 10).	Up to £1,000.
Failure to comply with the requirements of the investment gold scheme (FA 2000 s 137).	17.5% of the value of transactions concerned.
Import VAT (FA 2003 ss 24–41): —failures relating to non-compliance —evasion.	From 27 November 2003: maximum penalty of £2,500 maximum penalty equal to VAT sought to be evaded.
Failure to notify the use of a designated avoidance scheme (VATA 1994 Sch 11A paras 10, 11).	15% of the tax avoided (applies to businesses with supplies of £600,000 or more from 1 August 2004).
Failure to disclose certain schemes within 30 days of the due date or the first return affected (VATA 1994 Sch 11A paras 10, 11).	£5,000 (applies to businesses with supplies exceeding £10 million from 1 August 2004).

Index

A

Accounts, inheritance tax	
due dates	68
excepted estates	69
Advisory fuel rates	51
Age allowance	46
Aggregates levy	44
Agricultural buildings allowances	21
Agricultural property relief	70
Annual accounting scheme, VAT	88
Annual exemption	
capital gains tax	24
inheritance tax	68
Approval applications	20
Authorised mileage rates	51
Average exchange rates	76

B

Bank base rates	3
Basic rate of income tax	45
Basis of assessment	
employment income	56
overseas income	81
Benefits, employee	53–55
Benefits, social security	82, 83
Blind person's allowance	46
Bus services	49, 53
Business property relief	70

C

Capital allowances	
agricultural buildings	21
claims, time limits	17
conversions into flats over shops, etc	21
disadvantaged areas	23
dredging	21
elections, time limits	17
enterprise zones	23
films	21
flat conversions	21
industrial buildings	21
know-how	21
machinery and plant	22
mines and oil wells	23
patent rights	23
rates	21
renovation of business premises	23
research and development	23
scientific research	23
Capital gains tax	
annual exemption	24
chattel exemption	24
claims, time limits	16
due date	4
elections, time limits	16
exemptions	24, 28
hold-over relief for gifts	28
indexation allowance	25, 30
interest on overdue tax	5
leases	27
penalties	12
personal representatives	29
rates	24
reliefs	28
retail prices index	42
retirement relief	28
returns, penalties	12
roll-over relief	2
share identification rules	25
taper relief	26
trustees	29
Capital goods scheme, VAT	90
Cars	
capital allowances	23
capital gains exemption	28
fuel for private use	
taxable benefit	50
VAT	91
hired: restricted allowances	49
private use	48
Cash accounting scheme, VAT	88
Certificates of tax deposit	11
Charities	
capital gains exemption	28
gift aid	52
gifts in kind	52
gifts to, inheritance tax relief	70
payroll giving scheme	52
Chattels, capital gains exemption	24
Cheap loans to employees	53
Child tax credit	67, 83
Claims, time limits	
capital allowances	17
capital gains tax	16
corporation tax	17
income tax	16
Clearance applications	20
Clearing houses	19
Climate change levy	44
Community investment tax credit	59
Company share option plans	66
Compensation, capital gains exemption	28
Computer equipment	55
Construction industry scheme	45
Corporation tax	
claims, time limits	17
corporate venturing scheme	43
due date	4
elections, time limits	17
interest on overdue tax	6
interest on overpaid tax	9
marginal relief	43
penalties	12
rates	43
reliefs	43
research and development expenditure	43
returns, penalties	12
Corporate venturing scheme	43
Customs levies and taxes	
aggregates levy	44
climate change levy	44
insurance premium tax	44
landfill tax	44
Cycles and cycle safety equipment	49, 55

D

Default interest – VAT	
VAT	92
Default surcharge	93
Deregistration limits, VAT	88
Disabled employees, equipment	54
Disadvantaged areas, capital allowances	23
Dividends	45
Double taxation agreements	
air transport profits	81
capital taxes	81
income and capital gains	79
shipping profits	81
Dredging allowances	21
Due dates of tax	4

E

Elections, time limits	
capital allowances	17
capital gains tax	16
corporation tax	17
income tax	16
Employees	
accommodation, supplies etc used in employment duties	53, 75
assets given to employees	53, 75
bus services for	49, 53, 55
car benefits	48, 75
cheap loans	53
childcare	54
Christmas parties and annual functions	53, 75
clothing and uniforms	75
computers provided for private use	55, 75
credit cards and tokens	75
cycles and cycle safety equipment	49, 55
disabled, equipment etc	54
emergency vehicles	49
entertaining	75
expenses, fixed rate allowances	54, 55, 58
eye tests	54
fixed-rate expenses	57
fuel benefits	50
holidays	75
homeworkers	54
incidental overnight expenses	54
living accommodation	54, 75
living expenses	54
loan benefits	53, 75
long service awards	55
meals	55, 75

medical check-ups and insurance	55, 75
mileage rates	51
mobile phones	55
national minimum wage	56
notional payments	75
parking facilities for	49
payments in kind	75
personal expenses	55, 75
prize money	75
relocation benefits	55, 75
round sum allowances	75
scholarships and school fees	75
services supplied	75
share schemes	65
tax paid for	75
telephone costs	75
third party gifts	55
use of employer's assets	55
van benefits	49
vouchers	55, 75
Employment income	56
due dates of tax	4
Enterprise investment scheme	
capital gains exemption	28
income tax relief	59
Enterprise management incentives	65
Enterprise zones	21, 23
Excepted estates, inheritance tax	69
Excepted transfers	69
Exchange rates	
average	76
year end	78
Executive share option schemes	66
Exempt supplies, VAT	90

F

Fixed rate expenses	57
Flat conversions, capital allowances	21
Flat rate scheme for small businesses, VAT	89
Foreign exchange rates	
average	76
year end	78
Foreign income	
basis of assessment	81
employment income	57
Foster carers	61
FOTRA securities	81
Fuel for private use	
income tax	50
VAT	91
Futures exchanges	19

G

Gift aid	52
Gifts in kind	52

H

Hired cars and motorcycles	49
Hold-over relief for gifts	28
Hotels, capital allowances	21

I

Income tax	
claims, time limits	16
due dates	4
elections, time limits	16
interest on overdue tax	5
lease premiums	27
penalties	12
personal allowances	46
rates	45
reliefs	46, 61
returns, penalties	12
Indexation allowance	25, 30
Individual investment plans	60
Industrial buildings allowances	
enterprise zones	23
rates	21
Inheritance tax	
agricultural property relief	70
annual exemption	68
business property relief	70
charitable gifts, exemption	70
due dates for accounts	68
due dates for tax	4
excepted transfers estates and settlements	69
gifts, reliefs	70
interest on overdue tax	7
marriage gifts, exemption	70
penalties	13
political parties, gifts exemption	70
potentially exempt transfers	70
quick succession relief	70
rates	68
small gifts exemption	70
tapering relief	70
Insurance premium tax	44
Insurance premiums, life	46
Interest rates	
bank base rates	3
capital gains	5, 8
certificates of tax deposit	11
corporation tax	6, 9
default, VAT	92
due dates	4
income tax	5, 8
income tax on company payments	7
inheritance tax	7
national insurance contributions	5, 8
official, cheap loans	53
overpaid tax	8, 92
stamp duties	5, 8, 86
unpaid tax	5
VAT	92
Investment exchanges	19
Investment reliefs	
community investment tax credit	59
enterprise investment scheme	59
individual investment plans	60
National Savings Bank interest	60
personal equity plans	60
tax-exempt special savings accounts	60
urban regeneration companies	59
venture capital trusts	59

K

Know-how, capital allowances	21

L

Landfill tax	44
Landlord's energy-saving allowance	61
Leases	
depreciation table	27
premiums	27
stamp duties	84, 85
Life assurance premium relief	61

M

Machinery and plant allowances	22
cars	23
rates	22
Maintenance payments	61
Marginal relief, corporation tax	43
Marriage gifts, inheritance tax relief	70
Married couple's allowance	46
Mileage allowances	51
Mines and oil wells, capital allowances	23
Minimum wage, national	56
Misdeclarations, VAT	93
Mobile phones	55
Motorcycles	51

N

National insurance contributions	
employers' contributions on benefits	75
interest on overdue contributions	5
interest on overpaid contributions	8
rates	71–74
National minimum wage	56
National Savings Bank interest	60
Nazi persecution, pensions to victims	81
Non-corporate distribution rate	43
Non-domiciled individuals	
employment income	57
overseas income	81
spouses, inheritance tax	70
Non-residents	
employment income	57
overseas income	81

O

Official rate of interest, employee loans	53
Overseas income, basis of assessment	
employment income	57
overseas income	81

P

Parking facilities	49
Partial exemption, VAT	90

Patent rights, capital allowances	23
PAYE	
penalties	13
weekly and monthly thresholds	56
Pay and file	
due date of tax	4
interest on overpaid tax	10
Payroll giving scheme	52
Penalties	
corporation tax returns	12
inheritance tax	13
interest on	15
mitigation of	15
PAYE returns	13
personal tax returns	12
special information returns	14
stamp taxes	86
VAT	93
Pension provision	
from 6 April 2006	62
personal pension schemes	63
retirement annuities	64
to 5 April 2005	63, 64
Personal allowances	46
Personal equity plans	60
Personal pension schemes	62, 63
Personal representatives	29
Plant and machinery allowances	
cars	23
rates	22
Potentially exempt transfers	70
Premiums on leases	
capital gains tax	27
income tax	27
stamp taxes	84, 85
Profit sharing schemes, approved	66
Property income lease premiums	27

Q

Qualifying corporate bonds	28
Quick succession relief	70

R

Rates of tax	
capital gains tax	24
corporation tax	43
customs duties and levies	44
income tax	45
inheritance tax	68
stamp taxes	84, 85
VAT	87
Real Estate Investment Trusts	43, 45
Recognised clearing houses	19
Recognised futures exchanges	19
Recognised investment exchanges	19
Recognised stock exchanges	18
Reduced rate supplies, VAT	90
Registration limits, VAT	87
Reliefs	
capital gains	24
corporation tax	43
income tax	46, 61
inheritance tax	70
Remission of tax	7
Renovation of business premises	23
Rent, stamp duties	84, 85
Rent-a-room relief	61
Repayment of supplement VAT	92
Research and development	23, 43
Retail prices index	42
Retirement annuities contracts	63
Retirement pensions	62–64
Retirement relief	28
Roll-over relief	29

S

Save as you earn (SAYE) share option schemes	65
Savings	45
Scientific research allowances	23
Securities, tax-free for non-residents	81
Share identification rules	25

Share incentive plans	65
Share schemes	65
Small companies' rate	43
Small gifts relief	70
Social security benefits	
non-taxable	83
taxable	82
Stakeholder pensions	63
Stamp taxes	
conveyances or transfers	85
disadvantaged areas	84
exemptions	84
fixed	85
interest	86
land transactions	84
leases	84, 85
penalties	86
premiums	84, 85
rates	84, 85
reliefs	84
rent	84, 85
repayment supplement	86
rounding	85
stamp duty land tax	84
stamp duty reserve tax	85
stock transfers	85
State benefits	
non-taxable	83
taxable	82
Stock exchanges	18
Supplement VAT	92

T

Taper relief, capital gains tax	26
Tapering relief, inheritance tax	70
Tax credits	67
Tax-exempt special savings accounts	60
Termination payments	56
Toll roads, capital allowances	21
Trustees	
capital gains annual exempt amount	24
expenses allowable for CGT	29
Trusts	
income tax rates	45

U

Urban regeneration companies	59

V

Van, employee benefit	49
VAT	
annual accounting scheme	88
capital goods scheme	90
car fuel for private use	91
cash accounting scheme	88
default interest	92
default surcharge	93
deregistration limits	88
evasion	93
exempt supplies	90
failure to notify liability	93
flat-rate scheme for small businesses	89
interest on overpaid tax	92
misdeclarations	93
partial exemption	90
penalties	93
rates	87
reduced rate supplies	90
registration limits	87
supplement VAT	92
zero-rated supplies	90
Venture capital trusts	
capital gains exemptions	28
income tax reliefs	59

W

Working tax credit	67, 83
Workshops, capital allowances	21

Z

Zero-rated supplies	90